MINDSET METHODS & METRICS

MINDSET METHODS & METRICS

Winning As A Modern Real Estate Agent

Brandon Doyle, Nick Dreher and Marshall Saunders

RockPaperStar Press, Minneapolis

RockPaperStar Press
333 Washington Ave. N.
Minneapolis, MN 55401
612-349-2744
www.rockpaperstar.com

ISBN-13: 978-0-9835887-7-1
LCCN: 2016905179

Distributed by Itasca Books

Illustrated by Corey Collins
Typeset by Alexis Cooke

Printed in the United States of America

Dedication

We dedicate this book to the real estate agent.

You are the bedrock of entrepreneurialism. You demonstrate every day the very best of self-reliance, hard work, and customer service. You rate below politicians and used car salespeople in every poll of "who do you trust," yet you soldier on, knowing that the vast majority of your potential clients think they know more about real estate than you do.

When the economy is good, your job is seen as superfluous and your advice of restraint is ignored. When the economy is bad, you are blamed for the unrestrained greed that led all the lemmings off the cliff.

You work when everyone else has time off, and then you work while everyone else is at work. Your job does not end at 6 p.m. It doesn't even end when you're asleep at night.

Your job never stops...until it stops. When the phone stops ringing and the buyers stop buying and the sellers stop selling, you are out of an income. Not out of work, just out of an income. Then you pray and work as hard as you can to get back to the point where you're working around the clock to please your clients and jumping right back on the hamster wheel.

You are the ultimate paradox. You want to be less busy and pulled in a thousand directions, and then the moment you get that break you so desperately wanted, you panic that you're going out of business.

You've sat at the kitchen table listing presentation and heard stories of bankruptcy, foreclosure, divorce, marriage, kids and retirement. The people across the table have cried, laughed, said awful things about you and your business, had totally unrealistic expectations...in other words, they have been totally and completely human, and you've seen it all.

We've been there. We understand. To you, we dedicate this book.

Contents

PART II: METRICS

Planning and Tracking for Success

PART III: METHODS

Growing your world of referrals, leads and contacts

An Introduction From The Authors

Being a real estate agent is, in my humble opinion, *the* purest expression of American entrepreneurialism. The real estate profession has everything:

- Helping clients achieve the American Dream of home ownership
- The opportunity to forge a successful career from sheer tenacity, street smarts and drive
- Anyone, regardless of race, religion, nationality, gender or economic background, can become a real estate agent—just pass the licensing exam and go out and do it.

There is no glass ceiling in real estate. In the 1970s, the real estate industry was flooded with success-minded women whose husbands were out of work or under-employed. In the field of residential real estate, these women found that their abilities to relate to clients, stage a home to sell, negotiate, and market could lead to a six-figure income—a salary earned by only a fraction of one percent of female executives at the time. Since then, we have witnessed a similar scenario play out with a number of other groups not otherwise granted ready access to the halls of American power and success, including African-American, Hmong, Somali and Latino real estate agents.

There are vast opportunities to be found in a residential real estate career. There are some hidden downsides, however. Whether encountered early on, or years into a career, such drawbacks can derail even the most determined entrepreneurs. These are the challenges that this book seeks to address. With proper outlook, motivation, planning and execution, the typical pitfalls of residential real estate can be lessened, if not avoided altogether.

Chief among these hazards is the problem of work/life balance. I remember when my daughter, Calla, was six months old, and I was feeding her solid food for the very first time. I held the baby spoon, heaped with Gerber Squash, and directed it toward Calla's little mouth, trying to hit the target while avoiding all her other wriggling parts. I managed to get as much on her face, hands, and neck as in her mouth, but what a great moment for a dad!

This special memory is marred, however, by what happened next. We were interrupted by a phone call from a client, who demanded that I drop what I was doing and race across town to show a property. When I declined to do so, he accused me of being a terrible agent. "I'll just find someone else!" he screamed, as he slammed down the phone.

I was crushed. And genuinely confused as to how I could make this all work. I looked at my daughter, no longer with the joy of the moment, but with the worry of paying bills that in this field who could benefit from what I've figured out. There is a *lot* of advice out there in the real estate world, but not necessarily a lot of quantified guidelines of the sort that I believe truly help to attach efforts to outcomes. Too many people are still working inefficiently, burning themselves out with time-consuming endeavors that yield unpredictable results.

My goal in co-writing this book is to help real estate agents get out of this rut, to run their businesses more efficiently, more predictably and more successfully. I am convinced that by implementing the right kind of focused and measured efforts—that is, the strategies that fit and make the most sense for *you*—anyone who wants to can have reliable success in their real estate business.

--Brandon Doyle

Why You Should Read This Book

If you've picked up this book, more than likely you're either contemplating, or have already undertaken, a career in real estate. Perhaps you've been working in the field for a year or two, or even ten or 20. There's a lot that you already know about the nitty-gritty of listing properties and handling closings, the details of real estate purchases and sales, working with a brokerage. You feel you're definitely on your professional way.

But, still. You have the sense that there's more you could be doing, or perhaps a more efficient way of doing what you're already doing...if only you knew what would work, and how well. For sure, you could be having better results—more clients, better listings, making more money. Maybe you're *OK*, but you really want to be doing ***so much better***.

Or, possibly, you're even feeling a bit demoralized. You really believed you'd be in a stronger position by now. You're willing to do what it takes, but *aren't quite sure* what to do next. You've been spinning your wheels, chasing after business, but without any cohesive method to your approach. The last thing you need is another story of someone else's success that offers nothing particularly meaty for you to incorporate into your own professional efforts. What you need is **an actual system to follow** that will help you clarify and achieve your goals.

Congratulations, you have come to the right place!

As real estate professionals with a combined 45 years' experience in the field, we are excited to offer you some guidelines you can use to build on what you've started, and to grow your business into the secure and reliable income stream that will weather market fluctuations. Anyone can sell in a hot market. What you need is a pathway to top-earning stability, whatever the economic climate.

If you're like most real estate professionals, you've attended countless seminars, and this certainly isn't the first book you've looked to for help. We've noticed that too many of the resources we've turned to for guidance in growing a real estate career are woefully deficient in actual useful content. The real estate world does not need another vanity project passing itself off as a "must-read!"

As we've developed winning strategies over the years, we've shared them with colleagues and brokerage partners through presentations and workshops. From the feedback we've received, we determined that maybe the real estate world does, in fact, need one more book. One that actually provides a **comprehensive system**, encompassing how to think (Mindset), how to plan, track and quantify efforts and outcomes (Metrics), and what actions to take (Methods). A system that will allow you to manage your real estate business and create the kind of growth and stability you truly desire.

We call our system **M³** ("M-Cubed"), a catchy name intended to get you thinking about the importance of each "M," as well as the exponentially greater power of all three components working together. With the right Mindset, data-driven Metrics, and structured Methods, you will be able to design the real estate business you want, and live a life you enjoy. It does require work, and it won't always be easy. But if you follow the **M³** formula, we are quite confident that you will see the results of your dreams.

PART I

Mindset

The Foundation of a Top Producer

Chapter One:
The Big Picture

The profession of real estate is extremely easy to enter, but for most people, a very difficult profession in which to succeed. It is a structure that entices the many and rewards the few. Selling homes and commercial properties attracts people from all backgrounds, all ages, all educational levels, in every imaginable demographic niche. We know that great income can be made in this line of work, because of high profile industry representatives, HGTV, the overall high price of homes, and because your real estate agent friend told you so. And, doesn't everyone want a flexible schedule?

In reality, attrition in the real estate profession is high. People move in and then quickly out when it turns out that excessive effort and unreliable income, coupled with an unsupportive environment, keep sustainable success at bay. The broker system is set up to help establish new agents, but often only to a limited level of success. Individual agents are typically discouraged from growing their business beyond certain limits, as many brokers feel threatened by an agent's independent success.

Brokers provide some entry-level education to those new to the real estate industry. However, agents often find themselves unsure how to proceed and truly succeed. In an atmosphere of continual struggle, with few measurable directives, generic suggestions such as, "Develop your Facebook page," "Have more open houses," or "Write a blog" can feel like being told to throw some spaghetti at the wall and see what sticks.

Without a cohesive structure, an actual formula connecting X + Y to equal Z (with Z being income), it's impossible to understand how much of any specific efforts, or what combination of several, will yield actual results. Selling real estate this way appears to be nothing more than hocus-pocus.

Many agents thus come to believe that *the market* is what leads to success or failure. That their livelihood hangs in a continual fragile balance dependent upon factors outside anyone's control. Most agents, even those who enjoy fruitful years, live a mere three months from bankruptcy if the market should grow cold and they find themselves without a sale for an extended period of time. Few have significant savings, or plans for retirement.

It is no surprise that this economic and professional instability causes extreme levels of stress. Too often, the response is to either double up on the *quantity* of efforts, without knowing how those efforts might help, or declaring the profession unworkable and quitting. This leads to more instability and more stress.

***This is completely unnecessary*.**

We want to offer another possibility. If nothing else, we want you to have this takeaway: **It is possible** for you to:

- get a handle on your real estate career,
- treat it like the business that it is, and
- engage in structured efforts that will generate *exactly* the results you set out to achieve.

Not only is this a fact, but we are going to explain to you *how* to do it. Having a successful real estate business is not magic, nor is it based on luck. It is based on diligent efforts, continual monitoring, and knowing your numbers. You'll have to do the work, but you can know precisely what work you need to do. No more spaghetti. Just reliable methods and analytical metrics.

But first, you gotta get your head in the game. There are a number of mindset adjustments that will set you up to be thinking for success.

Mindset Principle #1:

Real Estate is a Business. Run Your Business Like a CEO.

You kind of already know you run your own business, because you don't have a boss, and no one else is paying you a salary. It's on you to cover the expenses you incur, and you make your own schedule. Also, you've taken some seminars on developing your real estate business.

But are you running your business like a CEO? Do you have a business plan? A marketing plan? Do you keep spreadsheets, track cash flow and expenses, review quarterly profit-and-loss statements? Most significantly, do you approach each fiscal year armed with a plan for how much business you will bring in, and precisely what you will do, and how much time and money you'll spend, to make that happen?

If you answer 'no' to any (or all) of the above questions, you are not alone! Taking your real estate business to the next level will likely require a shift in your thinking. If you can see yourself as the CEO of your real estate company (you are!), it becomes easier to think of your business development efforts in terms of the bigger business picture.

In a traditional product-based business, you don't just start with the selling. First, the product must be designed, and then it needs to be manufactured. There's sourcing, packaging, distribution, marketing—a million details that require thought and attention (not to mention money and time) in developing a solid business foundation. It is critical that the business owner understand the market to whom they are selling, as well as the unique value proposition offered, or the business will not succeed.

While some of the steps may look different, this general structure applies to a real estate business as well. In the real estate industry, the product you are developing is your database—that is, your list of relationships. How you attend to this resource requires the same level of time and thought as a manufacturer would put into the design of a product.

Before we get to any of the specific tactics you'll need to employ, it is essential that you make this **mental shift.** Understand that you are the CEO of your professional real estate corporation, and that this business rests upon a constantly tended database of relationships. As CEO, executing the annual business plan and meeting projected business goals depends upon your nurturing and maximizing this database resource, as well as understanding your market and your unique value proposition.

Mindset Principle #2:
The Horizon Mindset

The second mindset adjustment that requires concentrating on the big picture is thinking *relationally* rather than *transactionally*. What this means is really focusing your mental picture. Not on the individual listing or sale or commission, but rather on the larger view of how transactions will naturally occur (and not occur) from within the well-tended network of relationships you maintain.

I think of teaching my daughter how to drive. New to the driver's seat, she clutched the steering wheel, and looked anxiously at the road just beyond the front of the car. Every second, something new came into her field of vision and she yanked at the wheel, resulting in a jerky, nausea-inducing ride.

I had her adjust her attention to the horizon, where her peripheral view would encompass the entire field of where we were going, as well as what was coming at us. Then she could see potential changes in the road long before we got there, so she didn't have to react in a panic, wasting energy and threatening our safety in a series of over-corrections. We began to drive in a smooth, straight path. It wasn't long before she was calmer, feeling more in control of the car, and more comfortable with the experience of driving.

Adjust your mindset. Train your gaze to look to the horizon, and commit to the long game of your real estate business, while taking specific, measured steps. You will be able to even out the sharp swerves of the uncertain, anxiety-driven reactive approach, in favor of the smooth, stable journey of a proactive approach. This shift makes all the difference. You become the master of your business, rather than its subject.

Mindset Principle #3:

Set Your Goals, Know your Numbers, Make it So

The third foundation of our big picture philosophy involves knowing where you are going. After all, it won't help you to look at the horizon if you aren't aiming for a specific point. You must know where you are, and where you want to go. Then, establish and adhere to strategies to get from here to there. Just like driving the car.

We'll teach you how to calculate both your annual revenue and the actions you need to take to meet that goal in Chapter 5. However, to establish the proper mindset for implementing our program, all you need to do at this point is embrace the principle of goal-setting. That is, unless you specify what you're aiming for, you'll only keep aiming at nothing – and hitting it.

If you can precisely (and ambitiously) declare where you're headed—that is, set a specific gross commission income goal for the year—you can work backward, using our formula, to calculate the number of qualified leads and substantive contacts needed to make that income (your *Metrics*). From there, you can break down your year, based on the business development strategies you choose, to determine exactly what you need to do each day. This plan is the measurable, quantifiable amount of effort you must undertake daily, monthly, and yearly to achieve your goal.

The final piece of this goal-directed mental adjustment

is that you must commit to a disciplined and consistent plan of action (your *Methods*). Having set the goal you desire to reach, calculated the number of substantive contacts required to meet that outcome, and laid out a plan for making the daily number, the follow-through is your foot on the gas pedal to move the car forward.

A successful real estate business really is not built by magic, or luck, or something other people can do but not you. There is no 'easy' button, but we can offer you a solid process of steps to take and data to track, so that you can build a goal-driven, quantifiable, stable real estate business.

Chapter Two: Train your Brain to think like a Top Producer

There's one thing that all superstars have in common. To reach the top of any profession or sport requires more than talent, intelligence, practice, luck, patience, or knowing the right people—though each of these will surely help! But what matters more than anything else is having ***the right mindset***. Those who perform at an extraordinary level, with a high degree of success, need to have their head in the right place to do so.

Your brain is the catalyst for all your activity. If you don't have that central command kicking out positive and effective messages, you'll soon find yourself heading down the wrong path. It may sound simplistic, but finding and maintaining the correct mindset is the hardest—and most critical—part of being a successful real estate agent and a successful entrepreneur.

Most top athletes, entertainers and business leaders have a team of supporters to help them keep their focus. Even a top CEO gets motivational direction from his or her board of directors, president, vice presidents, or other advisors. Top athletes get the same from coaches, team owners, captains, and fellow players.

But real estate is often a lonely job. It's usually you, and only you, psyching yourself up in the car before you go inside for a listing appointment. Even if you work with others, you're the lone player on the court (or, at the conference room table) when you meet with a buyer for the first time. Regardless of the size of your team, the number of assistants you have, or how much help you get from your manager and office staff, you have to have what it takes to face this job alone.

Mindset is your ultimate tool for success.

This is where brain training enters. There are several things to be aware of and practices you can undertake when cultivating the mindset of a real estate winner.

Garbage in = Garbage out

It's important to be mindful of the sources of stimulation and influence surrounding you, and to take control (to the extent that you can) of negative, hostile, or unhelpful input. Try to keep yourself free of unnecessary distractions and downers—those thoughts and ideas that can pull you away from your own confidence and happiness. It's amazing how toxic negativity can be.

One surprising source of powerful toxic negativity is right in your own living room. At the risk of saying something unpopular, we encourage you to stop–*right now!*–watching any and all cable news programs or political talk radio shows. These shows have only two things to sell: fear and anger. Similarly, stop reading divisive or salacious posts on Facebook, or in any news feeds. That stuff won't put you in the right and positive mindset to do business.

We promise that this won't make you one iota a less informed citizen. On the contrary, you'll probably avoid 99 percent of the erroneous information out there. This is not a politically-oriented strategy. Fear, anger, and demagoguery can be found at every political extreme in this country, and all types of it are unhealthy and unhelpful.

If you take this advice, we promise you: your perspective on the world will be better, your life will be happier, your energy will be lighter, and you will not even believe how much extra time you have in your life. When you allow the garbage that is entertainment masquerading as news (as well as complaining co-workers, negative social media conversations, and other hostile messages) into your brain, you will only create and spew garbage out. So, stop taking it in.

Let *positivity* into your brain. Have good music on your cell phone, ready to play when you're at work and in your car. Keep audio or video classes from industry leaders such as Brian Buffini, Tom Ferry, Joe Stumpf, or whoever most inspires you queued up and ready to play at a moment's notice. Never miss a chance to have something motivational, reflective or educational coming through your headphones or speakers and into your mind. When you allow inspiring and stimulating substance into your brain, you can't help but put forth the same.

Also, be okay with silence sometimes. Have you ever noticed that great ideas often come to you in the shower, or as you lie in bed before falling asleep, or just as you have woken up? These are the times when your mind is at rest, and not being bombarded with constant stimuli. Your brain has a moment to have its own inspirational thoughts. Take time for silence and self-reflection, and allow your own creativity to bubble up.

Immerse in Positivity

What do you say to yourself throughout the day? What is your internal dialogue? The aphorisms we see on magnets and internet memes seem so cheesy, and you might think you're above all that. But we beg to differ. Constantly bombarding yourself with positive, self-affirming messages is extremely important.

We can all visualize what life would be like if you heard nothing but "you're stupid," "you're ugly," "you can't," or "you won't," from the very day you were born. We would agree that a person subjected to that kind of pessimistic messaging would have so much negativity to overcome that any success or happiness in their life would be against the odds.

Yet, it's easy for us to pass off positive messages ("yes, you can," "you're beautiful," "you're smart") as hollow and useless. But in fact, continually feeding yourself positive messages is vital to growing your mind and trying new things. It enhances your courage, so that you're less afraid of failure, and thus willing to try new things.

Post positive messages on your bathroom mirror, or on your car's dashboard. Read all of the positive memes on Facebook, and scroll right past the darkly political posts. Listen to positive and uplifting CDs or MP3s in your car or on your headphones at work. Invite positive messages and sayings into your mind all day long. It works.

A truth of business is that *only through failure will you reach a higher level of success.* We would add: *only through the power of positive thought will you have the confidence to fail.* Failure (or, perhaps more accurately, the *willingness* to fail) is the ultimate gateway to a high level of success. It's important to stop thinking that just because something went wrong, you should quit. This is true for individual real estate agents, as well as brokerages or other organizations.

Consider the story of Tom Watson, Jr., who was President of IBM in the early 1970s, and the son of IBM's founder. Tom Watson, Jr. helped usher in the age of the personal computer, which changed the world as we know it. Anywhere from five to nine percent of IBM's revenue was put toward research and new projects every year, and most of those projects failed. One day, Tom Watson, Jr. called a vice president to his office to discuss a disastrous development project that lost IBM around $10 million. Expecting to be fired, the Vice President presented his letter of resignation. Tom Watson, Jr. just shook his head and said: "You are certainly not leaving after we just gave you a $10 million education."

An education. That's what failure is to the success-minded real estate agent. In 2011 and 2012, we were all just walking around dazed from of the meteor-strike that was the housing market crash of 2008 and 2009. Many real estate agents experienced shaky confidence from coming close to bankruptcy during the Recession. When anyone told me they felt they should quit the profession, I presented them this question:

> **"*Let's say you are flying in an airplane. An engine blows out. The pilot must know how to land the plane on one good engine. Whom do***

you want at the controls? The pilot who has been through a scary situation like this before, or a pilot who has learned emergency landings only in a simulator? ”

Wear your battle scars with pride.

Positive thoughts and adages help you cut the proper course in life. Your mind is a bit like a thickly overgrown jungle. You stand at the border of this jungle every day. You dive in and start hacking at the vines and the trees and the underbrush. Slowly but surely, you've hacked your way through the jungle. Then, the next day, you go the same route, except today is slightly easier than yesterday because there are fewer branches to cut and underbrush to chop. The next day is easier, and the next day easier still. Day after day, you walk the same path, until it's smooth and easy.

Your mind works the same way. The jungle of your mind is under constant bombardment from information, news, opinions, self-talk that you hear on a daily basis. As you chop through the underbrush, you're either creating a path toward a negative place, where you will see the worst in every situation and your goals will be left unfulfilled; or toward a positive place, where you reach your full potential and create the career and life to which you aspire.

Is your mental path taking you to a positive or a negative place? It's hard to retrain your mind. Once you've worn down a path, your mind will immediately take this easier course in whatever situation arises. If you don't like the path you've cut, you have to start chopping a new one. Listen to positive messages and read positive writings. Meditate, exercise, and spend time with positive people. All this will train your mind every day to do the tough chopping to create a new and positive pathway in your mind. Over time, this trail becomes more worn down and easier to follow, while your previous route slowly becomes overgrown, and fades in to the expanse of the jungle.

Take Time for Yourself

In the same spirit as making space in your day for positivity and creative thinking, make sure that you take time for yourself. This may take the form of vacations, or it could be regular visits to the spa for a massage or manicure. Maybe it means taking 30 to 45 minutes each day to read a good book, or for yoga. For some, time for oneself might be spent in prayer, righting yourself in your own spiritual connection to a higher being or power. Whatever the form, making time for yourself is an essential component to reaching the highest levels of success in real estate.

Real estate agents can often fall into the trap of thinking that being busy means being successful. Or worse, its corollary: *not* being occupied with a business-related activity every second of every day means being *un*successful. (We've all been there!) This is simply not true. In fact, the most prosperous real estate agents have well-managed schedules, with several times a day when their calendar is open!

Bottom line: you need to be in balance, *as you,* to be effective at running your business and your professional life. Be in touch with the good things that working hard provides to you and your family. Practice self-care, and you will be rewarded with more energy and enthusiasm for the time you do spend on work. When I stopped spinning my wheels, being busy for the sake of being busy, and started taking dedicated time for things that made me happy, my business was immediately more productive and successful.

Take Time for your Business.

Just as it's crucial to dedicate time to nourishing yourself, so too is it essential to devote time to focus on your business. A real estate professional should take a full assessment of their business, its direction and progression towards its goals, every six months. For me, this means taking business retreats, ideally twice a year, in the spring and in the fall.

I made a habit of attending my brand's annual convention every year in the spring. Sure, there were parties and social engagements, but I opted out of most of the frivolity, and attended education sessions each day. I had great conversations with agents from around the country between each session. Before the convention, I'd researched agents whose business I admired, and sent an invitation ahead of time, to meet and talk while we were both at the event.

This accomplished several things. For one, I got to know how other agents were running and growing their business in other markets, which provided me with a fresh source of inspiration beyond what I saw every day. People in different markets can be easier to talk to, and more open with their professional advice, since you are not perceived as competition. In addition, having conversations like this makes for great referral contacts. (We'll talk more about how to grow these referral contacts into a strong lead production component in Chapter 7.)

While other agents went out partying in the evenings, or participated in "rah-rah" sessions at the convention, I spent time in my room, or at a nearby coffee shop, reviewing my business plan. I'd start with a full assessment of the goals that I had made for the year: Where was I at? Was I meeting my benchmarks or not? What methods for business were going better than I had hoped, and which ones worse? Were there any activities that I should eliminate from my daily or weekly schedules, because they were failing to produce results? Should I implement some new strategies?

It was refreshing to ask myself these questions in the clear light of a dedicated business retreat. Entrepreneurs face so many emotions on a daily basis. You can go from having the world by the tail in the morning, to feeling like you're going out of business by lunch, then be confidently reassured by dinner, and go to bed wondering if you should apply for that restaurant management position. Each day, you're confronted with pin-balling feelings, as well as reactionary impulses. This is not the best climate in which to conduct business planning. These are the times that you *follow* a plan. No matter what, you get up each and every day, and follow the plan that you have made for your business.

Business planning, goal setting, strategy construction and selection cannot be done during the day-to-day battle of running a business. And yet, these are integral activities to your role as CEO of your business, and to creating a stable platform from which to grow.

Plan to plan. That is, set aside a chunk of time, ideally in a physical location away from your daily life. Turn off your phone, and give your business your full attention. This is the very definition of "getting outside of your business." After you've taken the time to get a solid handle on where you've been, where you're going, what you've done with excellence, and what needs a bit of course correction, you can drop back into your daily work life with greater confidence, clarity and effectiveness.

Your Business Should Be Bigger Than You

Some people (though we'd argue not many) can perform this kind of regular business assessment without physically leaving town, or without even removing themselves from their office. I'm not one of those people, and I'm not sure you should be, either.

I use the word "retreat" intentionally—I back away from my business. For me, the act of flying in an airplane to go to my business retreat, and then flying back home afterward, signaled something in my brain. The physical separation allowed me to create a psychological separation as well. Being at least several hundred miles away, if not a thousand, helped me to look at my business from a distance, and to see it realistically and holistically.

I did all I could to separate myself from the business at these retreats. I'd hand over my clients to other agents and assistants, and demand that I only be reached if something truly needed my assistance. This activity in itself taught me several things.

#1

True business leaders strive to replace their abilities and positions within their organization.

Often, real estate agents want to do everything, and trust only themselves to perform every task of their business, out of a misconception that singular responsibility proves their worth and necessity. The old adage *if you want something done right, you have to do it yourself* is dead wrong. If you really must do everything yourself for it to be right, then you haven't found the right staff, partners, or team to work with you, or you haven't educated your clients on how you manage your business.

Some agents do every single task because they are threatened by the idea of someone else being able to do what they do. The disastrous effect of this attitude is that it stifles the potential growth of their business by limiting it to only the amount they can personally cover. It also limits them by demanding that they be 'on,' or at least on call, every minute. It's hard to block out personal time when there's no one else to step in, should an issue come up.

The more effective approach is to always be striving to create a business that can run seamlessly *without you*. Of course, you provide the passion and direction and overall operational know-how. But to truly have a successful and growing business, it should be able to run without your daily input or physical presence.

#2

Run your business like you're always leaving town next week.

You know how it goes: you could be twiddling your thumbs for weeks, but the moment you leave town, everything seems to need attention. New buyers crawl out of the woodwork, sellers want to list, and every closing seems to be a train wreck.

Some of this can be chalked up to good old-fashioned bad luck. But often, something deeper is going on. Think of what you do the week before you leave town: you call all of your sellers, make sure everything is okay with them, and try to tie up loose ends; you do the same with buyers, and with the lenders and closers on the transactions you have lined up to close. You're calling, emailing, and otherwise touching base with every active client that you have at the moment. You are whipping up activity.

This activity comes bears fruit through questions and renewed interests and concerns. For example, a seller might have some lingering questions in the back of their mind about the level of activity on their listing. When you call to let them know you'll be gone next week, these concerns percolate to the surface. My dad always told me to leave town without telling anyone.

But on the contrary, we encourage you to operate in each regular week as if you *are* leaving town next week. Constantly touch base with clients and closers and lenders. Whip up the activity that you would have whipped up had you been leaving town. Then, when you are actually going to leave, simply slip out without anyone knowing. Again, this articulates the importance of having a business that can run properly without you.

#3

Constantly cultivate a great group of people that can help and support you when you are gone.

This is kind of like the first point above, but at a higher and more temporary level. Leaving town and your clients helps you to realize who you can trust to run your business. After all, you might have to leave your business for extended periods of time at some point, and you need to build an operation that can run itself to some degree.

An agent friend of mine was diagnosed with lymphoma, and had to undergo extensive chemotherapy. The treatments themselves took several weeks to administer, sidelining him from his business. But even worse was the physical toll the treatment and recovery took, leaving him frail and unable to fully work for months. His successful fight against lymphoma nearly ruined his business, despite the best efforts of his friends and family to fill in for him in his absence.

Don't ever have your business so dependent on your personal presence. Take less horrific examples: you break your leg, you want to visit a relative, or you simply want to have work-life balance. If you're continually building a strong cadre of people who can step in for you, you're developing a safety net for the inevitable.

The long and the short of it is: having a real estate business that is completely and totally dependent on you may make you feel needed and loved, but it will also make you a slave to your own business. Don't do this. You—and your business—

are better than that.

#4

Be willing to fire bad clients, even if you've worked very hard to get them.

There's a saying in management: *Be slow to hire and quick to fire.* This is also true in real estate, where it might take you weeks or months of exhaustive enticing and convincing to finally win that buyer or seller as your client.

Clients who don't appreciate you—or worse, actively work against you—make your job and your life miserable. Of course, try correcting them first (in a teacher/pupil way, not *The Shining* way). Sometimes, after you have outlined acceptable client-agent interaction, and declared your willingness to drop an uncooperative client, they'll straighten up and be more willing to work collaboratively with you. If not, break ties.

Too many agents make the disastrous decision to stay with a bad client because they've put so much time and effort in with them already. "I don't want to throw all of that away...and we are *so* close to the finish line" is an all-too familiar refrain. But take our advice: no matter what point you're at in the process, drop that toxic client, and *move on*. The energy you expend getting another client will be a much better use of your time, and much better for your mental health.

Keep Your Business in Balance

It's a common pitfall in the real estate industry to become overwhelmed by the pressure to respond to everything that seems urgent. Been there, done that! Surely, you've heard the saying *work smarter, not harder* a million times, but the practical application of this concept can be elusive. It is helpful to think of your business as a **three-legged stool**.

Agents too often see being busy as synonymous with being successful. But that is not always true. Think of a major business that sells to the public—let's take Apple, for instance. Apple has three fundamental parts of its business:

1. **The Headquarters**: Here, products are developed; strategies are mapped out; markets are researched; insights into customer preferences are charted, examined, and challenged; advertising campaigns are created; design work is done on products and packaging; etc.
2. **The Factory**: This is where the actual product is created. No matter how well the product is designed and marketed back at HQ, if the product is not made well in the factory, then the whole system falls apart. It's important that the factory very closely follow the designs sent to it from HQ, as they need to deliver exactly what was promised to the consumer.
3. **Shipping and Receiving**: This is where it all comes together. All of the design, marketing, planning, and manufacturing mean nothing if the product is not sold and delivered to the consumer. Maybe the product was ordered online and delivered by FedEx, or perhaps there was a retail store that the buyer walked into, received good help, and then made their purchase in person. However it happened, this final element is crucial.

These are three different and distinct elements of a

company, but none of them can be successful on their own. It's a three-legged stool, and thus it requires proper balance in the three aspects.

During the holiday season, Apple is surely bit busier in the shipping and receiving department than they are at headquarters. And there are certain times a year, perhaps after a new product launch, or in preparation for Christmas, that the factory is busy preparing the products for sale. There are times when the headquarters is in intensive sessions regarding planning and product development and marketing talks. Even though each division of the business has their busy and slow times, they must all be working together to make the operation successful.

In the business of the real estate agent, the same three divisions should exist.

The **headquarters for the agent** is where you perform business planning; adjust and review the business plan thoroughly at least twice a year; analyze your market and potential clients; develop marketing plans; adjust and perfect buyer and listing presentations and establish new prospecting tactics.

The **factory floor** is the conference room, or a client's kitchen table. Here, you produce representation contracts with buyers and sellers. You sign the paperwork through which you formalize the relationship with your client and guarantee your payment when a completed transaction is produced. It is on this factory floor that you fully engage your client in the process of working with you.

The **shipping and receiving department** for an agent can also be called **fulfillment**. It encompasses all of those activities that it takes to fulfill an agent's contractual duties: showing homes; writing up and negotiating offers; going to inspections; securing any needed city/county/state inspections; following the paperwork towards a successful closing; attending the closing; etc.

Most agents consider the activities associated with fulfillment as their main job. You must shift your thinking about this part of your process. The activities of fulfillment are simply the necessary steps taken to get a buyer contract or listing agreement to a successful conclusion. An agent who shows homes all day long may have certainly worked hard, but they may have ignored other equally important aspects of their business.

Yes, there are times when fulfillment is necessary. Just as the shipping and receiving department is busier during Christmas, the agent's showing activity is very high during the spring market. Would you imagine, however, that Apple, LG, GE, GM or any other major corporation totally shuts down their headquarters or factories simply because their shipping and receiving department is so busy at Christmas? That would be inconceivable and ineffective. Don't run your business like this, regardless of how busy you might be in the spring market. This is the definition of *working smarter, not harder.*

There's another saying that might be a bit overused and not that well understood: *Work on your business, not in your business.* It can be a bit of a head-scratcher. But, if we follow the metaphor above regarding the headquarters, factory, and shipping and receiving of your business, perhaps it will make sense.

The strongest real estate agents prioritize headquarters and factory activities before shipping and receiving. After all, if you aren't finding clients and marketing to them, and then creating a high quality product of which you are very proud, you won't get a chance to do much shipping and receiving in the future. Plan your weeks so that headquarters time is allotted properly. Then, leave open several times in the week to meet with clients to do the factory work. Then, go ahead and *fit in* time for the fulfillment work.

Planning and working **on** your business is not something you *fit in* around doing the work **of** your business. It needs to be the other way around. Doing the work of your business is something you *fit in* around planning and working on your business. This is the definition of *working on your business rather than in your business.*

Brain-Training Habits

The Mindset of a winning real estate agent can be reinforced by habits. Some everyday habits that can cultivate a more creative and deliberate mindset include:

- **Write in longhand as much as possible.** We have become very used to typing on a computer, and that is fine for most business activities. However, when journaling and business planning, it's a good idea to write things out the old-fashioned way, with a pen or pencil on paper. There is a science to this, as described in Daniel Kahneman's book *Thinking Fast and Slow*. When you write in longhand, it slows down your brain and your thinking. You automatically become more deliberate and reflective. It creates the perfect biorhythm for business planning and strategic thinking.

"

The Importance of Good Writing

While we're on the subject of writing, heed this advice: learn how to write as well as possible. You need not be the next Hemingway or Austen; just know that the power to succinctly put your thoughts down in writing is the most overlooked and underappreciated tool in the business world.

Get a quick boost in your writing skills by reading The Elements of Style by William Strunk and E.B. White (you know, the guy who wrote Charlotte's Web). In writing classes, this book is often simply called "Strunk and White." It's a short book – only 85 pages. As you read it, you'll learn how to have an economy with words. Your writing will be more effective and accurate. It's an important skill to have as a representative of other people's interests, and as a negotiator of said interests.

You may even find two bonus benefits in reading Strunk and White. 1) you'll be reminded of all those nit-picky grammar rules you were taught in 7th and 8th grade, which will help you correct everyone on Facebook; and 2) you'll study a book co-authored by a man who penned one of the greatest quotes about time management: "I arise in the morning torn between a desire to improve the world and a desire to enjoy the world. This makes it hard to plan the day." E. B. White would have been a good real estate agent! "

- **Journal every day - in longhand.** It is so important to take stock of your daily activities! Journaling can help you do this. Your entries don't have to be poetic or well-written, and they don't have to include especially deep or insightful thoughts. Just regurgitate on paper at least one paragraph about what you have done over the last 24-hour period.

  For me, it's best to have a journal like this right next to my bed, for writing in just before I go to sleep. Often, my journal entries trail off at the end with unintelligible scribble because I'm falling asleep while writing. (Note: I suggest that you use a pencil for these journal entries, as your writing instrument may get lost in your bedsheets when you nod off. Pens can be messy.) Each night, you can start by reading the previous day's entry. Keeping track of your daily progress toward your goals is an extremely important part of following a business strategy.
- **Read a little every day.** It might be your favorite real estate website, or a business book, but reading has much the same effect as writing longhand. It slows down your thinking. You become less reactive, and more proactive. Your brain reaches a higher level of functioning. Plus, it brings the added benefit of learning and growing as a human being.
- **Have a written business plan.** We can't stress this habit enough. Your business plan must be in writing, in your own hand. Write it in pencil, as any good business plan will be revised as the year goes on.

Your business plan is a living document. Don't just create it once a year, and then place it in a drawer where you never look at it again. Read the business plan, or at least part of it, *every working day*. Know it like the back of your hand, and live by its strategy on a daily basis. If, upon reviewing your business plan, you find it bears little resemblance to what you actually do on a daily basis, there is something wrong. Either you've created a plan that is out of synch with you and your business, or you have not developed daily step-by-step strategies for living by your plan.

Don't multi-task. It's a lie, all of it! People with many balls in the air are always in the process of dropping at least one. The only people who actually multi-task "well" are those who do everything incompetently in the first place.

Stop trying to do everything. Plan your days in advance, then follow your plan with discipline. Let staff, either your own or your broker's, take care of small things around the edges. Then, only do the next necessary task of the major project at hand. Don't take on more than one or two major projects a day.

By trying to do everything, you'll end up doing nothing, and looking foolish in the process. Be single-minded and focused. If you do, you'll be unstoppable.

The Economic Mindset of a Top Producer

Hold on, you're in for a bumpy ride!

My life changed when I was in Las Vegas for the 1998 RE/MAX International Convention. It was the last day of a four-day-long conference. Most people had left already. There was a session in a small meeting room on the top floor of the convention center, way in the back, with a speaker I had never heard of, named Brian Buffini.

I was instantly taken with him. Brian was funny and engaging in a way that grabbed me. He brought the real estate business, and the concept of working your sphere for referrals, into a new light for me.

Brian presented the intriguing suggestion that real estate agents should live their economic lives "backwards," as corporations do. That means the amount of money you make in any given day, week or month is saved and applied to your next fiscal year, and therefore should not affect your immediate lifestyle or financial choices.

It means rather than supporting yourself from what you're bringing in currently, you live instead on the commissions you earned *last year*.

How does it work? Starting on January 1, put every dollar you earn in commission this year into a money market account. Sometime in mid- to late-December, see how much you've amassed over the year. Take out the amount of money you need for the coming year to cover all your marketing, employees and business expenses. Divide whatever is left into 26 chunks. Each of these chunks will be a paycheck, which you pay yourself every two weeks.

You can have a payroll service do all of the work, and have your state and federal withholding taken out, just like you would in a "normal job." Now, you know exactly how much money you have to run your business, and you know your budget at home. It may seem relatively straightforward, but make no mistake - it can be tough to train yourself to live this way, and it requires immense discipline.

My wife has always been extremely supportive of my real estate career, but it hasn't always been easy for her. She grew up in a household where her father went to work for the state, every day, for 36 years. He left in the morning, and came home at night, and he had every night and every weekend off of work. He got a month of vacation, which he used throughout the year. He was off every single holiday, including Columbus Day and Veterans Day.

My wife was an adult, and married to me, before she knew what her father actually did for a living (reviewing contracts for the state Department of Economic Security), beyond simply "working for the state." Can you imagine your children not knowing you were a real estate agent? I know I can't.

Needless to say, the words "when are you getting paid next?" were never uttered in her household when she was growing up. To my wife, a job was where you went on a set schedule, and money was always provided to you regularly. Now, married to a real estate agent, her life had become very different.

For the first several years I was in real estate, she'd ask me "when do you get a paycheck?" I'd have to tell her it didn't work that way. Even worse were the times when I had a closing scheduled, only to have the closing be delayed, or my pay be subject to a "commission-ectomy" because I had to keep the deal together at the last moment. All of this perplexed and stressed my wife.

At the end of three full years in the business (which happened to coincide with my fateful trip to the RE/MAX Convention in Las Vegas in 1998), I had some tough choices to make in my career. Do I forge ahead, even though this business is taking a toll on my home life because of the long hours and unpredictable income? Perhaps a 9-to-5 job was in my future, with its predictable paycheck and free evenings and weekends.

It's impossible to imagine how my life might have gone had I chosen either of those extremes, but I can confidently say that both choices would have been wrong for me. I needed to create a third path.

After hearing Brian's advice about living on last year's commissions, I flew home to Minneapolis. On the flight, I laid out our economic reality. Together, my wife and I had $20,000 in savings and retirement accounts. It was early March 1998, and we had $5,000 coming in commissions before the end of March. We also had a baby on the way. By the time I landed, I had the entire plan mapped out.

My proposal went like this: We'd cash out of all of our retirement and savings. To that amount we would add the commissions coming to us in March, plus the money my wife earned from her job as a school teacher (which she would have through April, plus a maternity leave). We'd put all of that money into a pot, and that's what we'd live off of until the end of the year. All of my commissions that I earned between April 1 and December 31, 1998 would be placed into a money market account for use in 1999.

To my surprise, my wife was excited. She would pinch every penny, and make groceries and baby supplies, and stretch all other resources as far as possible. She actually enjoyed the challenge. She would rather have the drudgery of having very little than the anxiety of uncertainty.

We made it through the first year. I have to tell you, it was incredibly difficult to maintain discipline with this plan. There were months where we had very little on which to get by. It was incredibly tempting to see the money going into the money market and know that the only reason not to spend it was because of an arbitrary rule we had set for ourselves. We had to go without buying Christmas presents that year. No vacations, no movies, no extras. The irony was that during some of the tightest times in 1998, I was depositing $10,000 and $15,000 checks into my money market account, because my real estate business was going very well that year.

What an incredible feeling it was, when we got to the end of 1998, and started planning work and home budgets for 1999. We had put $180,000 away for the following year, *and* we had earned $2,700 interest at the same time!

The Backwards Economics method had several effects:

- 1. It had its primarily intended effect, which was to give us an **exact and predictable budget on which to live**. It allowed me to designate specific allocations for my business, and now, my wife could count on a "paycheck" every two weeks with the taxes already taken out. No more uncertainty.
- 2. An unexpected result was learning that I'm much **more frugal with amassed money** than I am when

spending money as it comes in. I analyzed and re-analyzed every lead program and CRM tool I had been using without a second thought for years. Now I took the time to consider the angles: where should I advertise? Should I have an assistant? How much should I pay an assistant?

↳ It's the salesperson's curse, right? Salespeople tend to be a bit loose with money, because we know we can always make more. Low on funds? Get out there and sell another home. It's our great asset, but it can also work against us. Under the retroactive budget plan, I stayed motivated by commission income, while I also knew exactly how much money I had to work with for the current year. It forced me to be smarter with every dollar, and to avoid the mentality that I could just make more money if I needed it.

↳ 3. My motivations became more aligned with what was best for my client. You may not ever intentionally put your own financial interests above those of your buyer or seller. However, your motivations should always be in alignment with your clients', not only to avoid conflicts of interest, but to avoid even the appearance of one.

We have all heard stories of real estate agents who have dropped a mortgage payment into the mail, knowing they'd be getting a commission check the next day. But what if that same agent is at the closing table the next day. As the massive mountains of paper are being passed back and forth, that agent notices something awry about the survey. The agent knows that bringing up this issue will surely delay this closing. If the closing is delayed, the agent's mortgage check bounces. If the agent says nothing at all, the closing proceeds and the house payment clears, (and hopefully the survey matter is cleared up after closing).

Whether the real estate agent was overtly acting in their own self-interest or not, they clearly had a financial interest in *not* bringing up the survey problem. What if the solution did not come so quickly after closing, or it even meant that the buyer purchased a home with a permanent or expensive encumbrance on their title?

When you're always making money for *next* year, these conflicts don't come up. The real estate agent does not have a financial interest in whether a closing happens today or a week from now.

When you put your client's needs above your own, you will earn a client for life. And rightly so, because by taking your own interests out of the picture, your attention—and integrity—are theirs.

Chapter 3: Understanding the Power of your Sphere

What is my sphere of influence?

If you've been in the real estate industry for any amount of time, you have heard the phrase "sphere of influence." Originally borrowed from the geo-political realm, it's become a concept ubiquitous to real estate professionals. For our purposes, your sphere refers to your capacity for influence and connections available with the people you know.

Your personal sphere includes your family, friends, colleagues, teammates, neighbors, kids' friends' parents, former co-workers, former classmates...in short, everyone you know by name. For most of us, this totals around 200 people. Luckily for you, this is a list you've been building your entire life. The people you already know are much more likely to give you a shot than a person you've only met once or twice.

It makes sense that the relationship-based real estate industry would be intimately familiar with the value of this large circle. Having a personal connection with someone, wherein they genuinely know (at least on some level) who you are, is the best basis for establishing a professional relationship. People want to work with people they **know, like and trust**, and the more *you* can be that person for more people, the better position you'll be in to grow your business.

Typically, depending on how you structure your business, between 65 percent and 80 percent of your income will come from your sphere of influence, so maximizing this resource is a no-brainer. There are ways to do this authentically, to nurture and grow your connections. There are also ways to *think* you are tending to your sphere that are actually less authentic, and therefore, less effective.

For example, many agents are attracted to automated so-called "efficiencies;" ways they can project themselves into the minds of people in their sphere with the touch of a 'send' button. Certainly there are ways to effectively use newsletters and email that can add value to your relationships. (See more on this in Chapter 6.) But the thoughtless overuse of email, particularly mass emails, is one of the *least* effective ways to connect with your sphere. If you're using this practice, it's a great place to start refining your approach.

Know, Like and Trust + Top-of-Mind = Sphere Sweet Spot

There are two key principles behind the strategy of building business from your sphere:

- 1. People want to work with people they **know, like and trust,** and
- 2. Clients will come your way when you are **top-of-mind** for those within your sphere.

Know, Like, Trust

First, let's talk about everyone's natural affinity for working with professionals they know, like and trust. It's kind of obvious, right? But when you work in a business like ours, which is so fundamentally based on relationships, it can actually become easy to overlook the fact that these connections require nurturing in a way that has meaning to each individual.

Agents are attracted to automation, and to ways that speed up their to-do list of making their contact numbers. This goes back to the transactional vs. relational mindset (discussed in the previous chapter). If you think of your contacts as numbers, you can cut a wide swath with one-size-fits-all messages. And you'll probably get an occasional hit from this approach.

But by doing that, are you really drawing upon the value of your position as someone people know, like and trust? If you're not making meaningful connections with those in your sphere, as individuals, it's possible you're actually being perceived as annoying. And that's wading perilously toward the shark-infested waters of being *dis*liked and *dis*trusted. Don't go there!

The people in our sphere are human, and—surprise!—like to be treated as humans. And everyone is a little bit different.

Take the time to find out what is meaningful for each person in your sphere, and approach them accordingly. Some people like to chat on the phone every so often. Some need face-to-face time. You may know people for whom it's important that you contribute to, or participate in, their favorite charity event. Some people desire more hands-on attention, while some actually prefer less. Facebook is popular for a reason—busy people can stay connected with their friends, from the convenience of their desk chair. But be careful how you use this tool—some in your sphere will completely avoid Facebook, and so your most excellent post would miss them entirely. Also, beware the social media time-suck—you can put in a lot of time with very little return. (For more on using social media to your professional advantage, see Chapter 6.)

The beauty of a personalized approach is that there are multiple mediums with which you can make your connections, and you can use some or all of them. Typical methods include personal phone calls, email, newsletters, in-person meetings, and social media. By incorporating a customized strategy, you will foster the core connection that people in your sphere have with you—that they do indeed know, like and trust you. This makes you the person they want to go to, or send their own sphere to, when it comes time to buy or sell a home.

And let's not overlook one of the great side benefits of taking a nurturing approach to your sphere connections: you strengthen your relationships with people you care about! That's not work, it's a mental health insurance policy.

Top-of-Mind

The second requirement for maximizing your critical sphere resource is that you must be the top-of-mind real estate professional to those within your sphere. Not just someone they really like, who can be counted on for amazing potato salad and a killer three-point shot, but someone who is *the best real estate agent* possible.

Research has shown that we have a limited capacity for brand recognition. In general, when it comes to real estate professionals, most of us max out around remembering one to three people. If you ask someone you know to name five real estate agents, they will probably be able to only give you half that many.

This means there is very little space on the mental hard drive for people to hold onto your name and professional awesomeness if you don't continually remind them of it. What it also means is that you don't need to take it personally that you have to do some reminding; it's just the way our brains work.

You never know when someone in your sphere will have the need to access that piece of information that answers the question: *who do I know that is a great real estate agent?* As a general rule of thumb, most people move every seven to ten years. Chances are very good that if you hang around someone for ten years, they will have need of your services at some point. Moreover, lots of people *they* know will be likely to need a real estate agent in that time as well. If you are the top-of-mind real estate agent for the person in your sphere, odds are strong that they will want to share you with others. Why? Because…wait for it…they know, like, and trust you!

Growing Your Sphere

Given that such a large portion of your business comes from your sphere, it's important to always continue to grow that list. Naturally, people will move away or fall out of contact. From a business perspective, that is okay, as long as you're able to make up any contacts lost. Ultimately, all of your marketing efforts should help *add* to your sphere of influence.

The most effective way to grow this list is to simply get in front of people and introduce yourself. Real estate is all about relationship marketing. (In Chapters 7 and 8, we discuss specific tactics to help you improve your relationship marketing, such as building a professional referral network and converting leads into appointments.)

Keep in mind that you'll have multiple categories of people within your sphere, describing not only *how* you know various groups, but also how *well* you know them. You'll want to tailor your communication approaches with people at different levels, and as your sphere grows and changes, some contacts will move around within your categories. People you bring into your sphere through outreach efforts may begin in a place where you have a more arm's-length connection, but the goal is to bring them closer over time. (For more about managing your database, see Chapter 6.)

Going Beyond Your Sphere

In addition to the 65 to 80 percent of your business that comes to you from your sphere, you'll need to capture that remaining 20 to 35 percent by drilling down into other sources of business. We've spent many combined years in this industry analyzing various methods of marketing to determine what practices provide the highest return on investment.

There are a variety of strategies for building your business beyond your sphere, and it's wise to consider as many as you can. However, we recommend that you not try to do it all, particularly at the outset. For best results, start with one or two options, selecting what is best for you. The approach you take will depend on your earning goals, your personality, and your strongest skills. It's best to master a single approach before adding more to your practice, allowing yourself to gain strength with focus.

Work your chosen approach(es) into your schedule and business practice for one entire year, in order to develop a track record. This will allow you to see how effective you've been, and to assess where your efforts have paid off. You'll also have some documentation regarding your costs relative to each transaction. As you begin to accumulate real numbers drawn from your own experience, you will be able to more closely tailor your plan for the following year.

Some people are inclined to switch gears when they think that what they're doing isn't working. Maybe it's been four months, and you've been working your internet referral strategy with textbook precision, to no avail. Just hang in there. While it's wise to remain open to course corrections along the way, don't jump ship too quickly. Constantly changing your strategy, or having an inconsistent strategy, is effectively no strategy at all. It is better to make small adjustments to the efforts in which you have already invested, so you can reap the rewards.

In the internet referral example, your long dry spell most likely means the return on investment is just around the corner. The numbers don't lie, and either you're due for success or you have the opportunity to evaluate what you aren't doing right. Either way, abandoning your approach at this point amounts to a waste of your time and effort, while staying with it is likely to pay off. As CEO, what makes more sense for your business?

Briefly, the methods we'll cover (in Chapters 7 through 11) include: social media, network referrals, internet leads, geo-farming, expired listings and FSBO, open houses, door-knocking, and home-buyer seminars.

We will provide insight on multiple marketing approaches that may work for you. There's no one-size-fits-all solution, and what works great for someone else may not be as effective for you. You will likely need to try out many different strategies in order to arrive at the approach and combination of efforts that get you to your goals. Our objective is to educate, inspire, and provide an array of tools you can use to become a highly successful real estate agent in your market. Ultimately, when you understand and refine your strategy, your success will belong to you, not to the randomness of the economy, and you'll be able to adjust to changes in market climate.

PART II

Metrics

Planning and Tracking for Success

Chapter 4: Starting Out—Tips on Planning

If you're just embarking on your real estate career, or perhaps anticipating a re-boot that will knock it out of the park, there are a few considerations that can help you start strong.

Choose the right brokerage for you

When starting out in the business, it's important to join a brokerage that matches your needs. There's no universal prescription as to how to do this. Many factors go into this major decision, and it's important to understand your needs.

For example, what in what stage is your career? How much training, mentorship and supervision do you want? Many of the larger brokerages will have training courses available to you, either free or for a fee. If you're in need of more hands-on training, look for a company that promotes teams and mentorship.

Brand awareness is a consideration that's important

when you're going after business outside of your own sphere of influence. Affiliating with a strong brand can lend you additional credibility. Choose a brand that compliments your niche. Research the area you'll be selling in, and see who has the most listings and sales. If relocation and out-of-state referrals are important to you, a brand with a national presence may be a better fit over a smaller local shop.

Ideally, your brokerage will have offices in the neighborhoods where you intend to focus, even if you plan to work from home. Visit multiple brokerages to get a feel for the culture. Talk to the brokers and agents. Sit in on a meeting or training, if possible. Gather information to help you put together a list of pros and cons.

Fee structure is important, and varies by experience and annual sales volume. Often, newer agents will only receive 50 percent of commissions earned, whereas experienced agents may get 90 percent or more. Be sure that you understand the fine print of fees and costs that are charged through to the broker. It's important to find out this information before you make any decisions, so you can make an apples-to-apples comparison of your options.

If you're considering a brokerage move, compare all of the fees side-by-side, and look at what would be your net take-home pay relative to your current income level. Also, create a sheet that compares different pros/cons of each company. After you've decided which cultural and brand factors are the most important for you, what remains will likely be an economic decision. The grass is not always greener—you will still be responsible for growing your business and generating leads. You will still be you, even at another company. Make sure you fully understand the choice you are making, and why.

At the end of the day, there are great agents who do a lot of business at every size and brand of brokerage. No single brokerage is necessarily better than another; you just need to find the one that works best for you.

Also, while you certainly want to represent your own brokerage in a positive light, *never belittle your competition.* Remember, real estate is a profession that thrives on strong, positive relationships. You may find yourself switching from one brokerage to another over the course of your career, and you never know who will bring the buyer for your next listing!

I was a broker for six years, with the largest RE/MAX franchise in the world. I have worked with, and consulted, many brokers across America and a few in Europe. I've been asked countless times: "Should I become a broker?" and "Should I stay a broker?" and "What makes a good broker?"

The answer to all three questions is the same: a good broker, and for that matter the *only* person who should consider becoming or remaining a broker, is someone who wants the success of their agents more than they want their own success. Just about every broker in the world *says* they want this, but only a few truly do.

When you're interviewing brokerages, ask the broker: "would you accept total financial ruin and physical pain if it meant the success of your agents?" If the answer is yes, then this is a broker to consider. No halfway intelligent person becomes a broker because they want a higher level of stature in an organization, or more financial success. Being a broker brings neither of these. Beware that such misinformation can be very attractive to narcissists and the unwise. This type of person is not the broker you want.

Truly great brokers wake up every morning and recite

Anthony Quinn's line from Lawrence of Arabia: "I am a river to my people!" Great brokers are servant leaders, who will subjugate their own personal wealth and recognition to the agents in their brokerage. True servant leadership is at the heart of every great organization. Brokerages, whether big or small, national brand or local, are no different.

I consider my father, Bill Saunders, to be one of these great brokers. He was a broker for 24 years before dying of colon cancer in 2008. Hanging behind his desk was an odd-looking diagram. Right next to the sweet picture of my daughter was a simple white square of paper depicting an upside-down pyramid. This, my father explained, was the organizational chart of a successful brokerage.

The broker held the very lowest position on this organizational pyramid. On the second level, above the broker, were the brokerage staff of accountants, managers, and front desk staff. The next level up was for the administrative assistants, marketing specialists, and showing assistants who helped the agents run their business. And at the very top level of the organizational pyramid were the agents, or the Sales Executives, as my father called them. These people claimed the most valuable level in the organization. It was the Sales Executive who was to be served in all ways, and at all times.

Visibly absent from this pyramid was the buyer and seller – the consumer. This was no mistake. In my father's model of a brokerage, the buyer and seller were customers of the Sales Executive alone. It was the brokerage's mission to help the Sales Executive and their staff to meet the needs of the buyer and seller. The relationship was between the buyer and the seller and their agent, rather than with the brokerage.

This bold concept was, and remains, very threatening

to the broker community at large. The broker community is consistently trying to create ties to the consumer, and to assert their supremacy in the consumer/broker relationship in order to maintain control and weaken the consumer/agent relationship. Brokers who adopt these tactics demonstrate their lack of a value proposition to the agent.

Just as every day an agent must win the business of a buyer and seller, every day a brokerage must win the business of their agents. "What have you done for me lately?" is not an unfair question for agents to ask. A successful agent must ask themselves: *Am I with the right team? Is my brokerage supporting me in every way possible through training, marketing, technology, and motivation? Is my economic arrangement with my broker fair? Is my broker in any way trying to assert a relationship with my buyer/seller to the detriment of my relationship with the buyer/seller?* It's the broker's responsibility to prove their value to the real estate agent every single day.

Find a Mentor

Working with a strong mentor early in your career will help to put you on a fast track for success. Whether you're a member of their team, or simply officemates, find someone who has already achieved what you want to do, and learn as much as you can from them. No one gets anywhere alone - disregard the folklore that we should all 'pull ourselves up by our own bootstraps.' The smartest and most successful among us recognize that it's foolish to waste time and energy reinventing the already very well-refined wheel.

I was very fortunate to have had my father as one of my best mentors. My dad taught me the art of negotiation, patience, and hard work. I'm continually learning new things from him, and I'm grateful for the insights his wisdom can offer me.

Another important mentor for me was a colleague from a brokerage where I worked when I was just getting started. Jeff Steeves saw potential in me, and gave me an amazing opportunity: to co-list a large number of properties with him. We partnered to go after additional business, and through trial and error, we worked to 'master the art of marketing.' Without Jeff's support and teaching, I wouldn't have been able to grow at the exponential rate that I did.

Even if you're not directly mentored by someone, look for successful agents around you, and study what makes them tick.

It can also be helpful to find trainers and online resources that will help you grow. I look up to speakers like Tom Ferry and Chris Smith, who each teach solid principals while leveraging the newest technology for efficiency.

When looking for mentors, choose someone with strong uplifting energy. It's been said that you are the average of the five people with whom you spend the most time. What does this mean? Think of the five people you see most often, and consider whether their attributes are the ones that you want to embody. The trait of negativity, for example, is a cancer that will spread and metastasize. Avoid associating with negative or critical people, and look for those who exude enthusiasm, positivity and a desire to help.

Remember that no one does anything alone. We all have to start somewhere, and we all need help. It's good career strategy to align yourself with smart and successful people who can help you achieve your goals. There are mutual benefits to these relationships, and one day, *you* will be in a position to mentor the next person. Pay it forward.

Plan your Schedule

Whether we like to acknowledge it or not, we all live by a schedule. It's on our minds all the time, and we are constantly glancing at clocks, phones or watches.

Remember when you were in high school, and you'd stare at the clock, willing the hands to move, to signal the end of the day, or freedom from a particularly boring class? Those final five minutes would pass *soooooo slooooooowwwwwlllllyyyy*, you could swear you saw the second hand tick backwards. This experience honed our awareness of time, and ever since, we've used the clock to organize our lives, and to count down the seconds until the arrival of something good–or something bad.

When you're working in real estate, time can be your friend or it can be your nemesis. You can use your flexible schedule to grab coffee with a friend, stop in for some groceries, catch up on your Netflix queue, get your hair cut. All important tasks, to be sure. But if you allow your so-called freedom to lead you from one 'important task' to the next, you can quickly find yourself at the end of a week having completed very little actual work.

Even more insidious is spending your time on tasks that *seem* like actual work, but are in fact a big drain on your energy and attention with little return. You know what we're talking about: unstructured Facebook time! Email! Those quasi-work-related endeavors that don't really contribute to your business success. Chatting with your co-workers and fellow agents in the office isn't getting you to a sale.

The solution to this time-management black hole? A

schedule! Take charge of your time, and make it work for you. The more you make it clear what you expect yourself to do, and when, the more you make it unthinkable that it won't happen. Seriously, it's that easy.

First, find a scheduling device that works for you. It could be iCloud Calendar, Google Calendar, the calendar on your favorite CRM tool, or a good old Franklin Planner. If you're a fan of digital devices, great! Use one. If you staunchly adhere to the paper-and-pen method, go for it! You need to determine what system will get you to record, consult, and rely on it, *religiously*, maintaining every single thing you do each day with documentary efficiency. Whichever method achieves all that? *That* is the one for you!

I like to use a calendar method that color-codes my activities. Everything, from working out to working on my database, has a different color. Whatever calendaring method you choose, you have to habitualize its use. Do what your calendar tells you to do, and tell *everything* to your calendar.

I can feel your resistance—*no, I will not be a creature controlled by my calendar!* But the funny thing is, it's just the opposite: your calendar will set you free! Once you have used your calendar as the great repository of all things time-determined in your life, you are *free* from having to keep the 500 different schedules (work, home, soccer, gymnastics, workouts, yoga, etc.) straight in your brain. Record events in your calendar as soon as a new commitment comes up, and you'll immediately be on top of conflicts and commitments.

I came to the real estate industry from a structured job, where every day was the same. There was a designated start and end time, and an expectation of what you should be doing throughout the day.

With real estate, you truly are your own boss, and will reap what you sow. This business requires a high level of discipline, and personal time management. If left unchecked, I could (and have!) spend hours of unproductive time on Facebook. Many agents stay busy doing busywork, and forget to do the things that are the most important: prospecting and face-to-face time with clients.

Outlook has been a life-saver for me. I simply block out time each day for every activity that I know I need to get done. I schedule all of my appointments in Outlook, and my phone reminds me where I need to be and when it is time to leave.

You now have freed up an amazing amount of bandwidth in your head. All kinds of creative and strategic thoughts are available to you when you're not focusing every synapse on remembering what time you need to be where. Get it on the calendar, and let it go.

Start with yourself.

First, record in your calendar everything that you need to do to be a healthy, balanced human being. You want to work out three times a week at your gym? Put it down. Take a run every third morning in preparation for your first 5K? Put it down. Appointments with doctors, hairdressers, kids' teachers? Put 'em down. Meditation time, Thursday happy hour, massage—whatever it is that you aren't really your best you without—make time for it by saving space in your week.

Move on to family life appointments.

Soccer games, special meals, eating at least three breakfasts with your kid a week. Put them all down in your Life Management Partner (aka, "calendar"). Even include special times to walk in the park with your dog and your son, or a date to check out thrift stores with your best friend. Put it all down.

Recording these appointments does not mean things can't happen spontaneously. From time to time you'll find an opening in your schedule, and you can just grab the leash and go. But putting these things into your calendar makes them a priority when your schedule inevitably becomes hectic.

Even planning goofing-off time, such "Lie on the couch and watch a movie," is a good thing to do. This does two things for you: 1) it prioritizes fun and relaxation for you alone and with your family and friends, and 2) it gives your mind permission to take these moments of relaxation. Because it is officially *on your schedule*, you are free to enjoy this moment of respite. It may seem unnecessary at first, but it works.

Now, business.

Here's where we start to get into the **metrics** part of our **M³** formula for growing your real estate business. How you schedule your work time is key to developing the habits and practices that will create your business success. The more you can train yourself to simply do what you have in your schedule, the more likely you will be to reap the rewards of consistency.

Left to your own devices, it can be too easy to convince yourself that you were sitting at your computer working when you were actually shopping online for shoes. But give yourself a specific assignment with a time commitment? Shoe shopping is not an option right now.

- 1. Schedule time to work on your database for **40 minutes every other day**.
- 2. Schedule **30 minutes every morning** to send out handwritten notes (we'll address this more later).

- 3. Schedule **20 minutes a day** to concentrate on social media. (For example, visit Facebook Sundays, Tuesdays and Thursdays; LinkedIn on Mondays and Wednesdays; and Twitter on Fridays. Again, more on this later.)

There may be other small items to put on your calendar for business. An example would be a once-every-three-week mailing. These are really difficult and time-consuming to do all at once. But if you schedule **15 minutes once every other day** to work on your mailing, you'll chip away at what otherwise might be an all-day project. One day, print half the letters. Two days later, you print the other half. Two days after that, you print the first half of the envelopes, and two days later you print the other half. Every other day for two weeks after that, for 15 minutes a day, stuff the envelopes and stamp them. It can be very difficult to find four or five straight hours to get out a mailing every three weeks. It's much easier, and a better use of your time and energy, to spend 15 minutes at a time on this activity. It's easy if you schedule it in, and then follow your schedule rigorously.

Once these small portions of your day have been scheduled, it's time to calendar the **bigger chunks**:

- Start with meetings that have been set up, including business lunches or dinners.
- Next, add one-and-a-half or two-hour blocks devoted to prospecting and growing your database. I like to schedule these blocks at least four days a week (I take Friday, Saturday and Sunday off from this type of prospecting), and I usually do a session in the morning (say, 9:30 a.m. to 11 a.m.) for prospecting, and one in the afternoon (say, 2:30 p.m. to 4 p.m.) for follow-up. This schedule is fluid, and I can drag and drop things if

I need to, but once it's on the schedule, I'm more likely to do it.

Now, your calendar is looking like a patchwork quilt, with all of your color-coded events filled in for the week. It's important to realize at this time that schedules are not fixed, immovable sculptures set in stone. They are changeable. A reflection of your commitments that may also yield to emerging priorities and new information.

Your schedule can be moved and squeezed when necessary. A good schedule helps us prioritize events. Perhaps an important client meeting pops up in the morning during a time that I have scheduled for a workout. I want to do both, but the client event has to take priority. I simply move the workout to another morning, or maybe later that day.

In some cases, I have to cancel that workout altogether. It happens. But even so, the calendar reminds me of my priorities, and what needs to be moved and rescheduled. Cancelling a workout that was written into my calendar provides a visual reminder of any divergence from my plan, as opposed to the more ephemeral feeling of accomplishment that comes from *thinking about* working out. And when something like a workout does have to fall by the wayside, having the next one already on the schedule keeps me from losing momentum.

Keeping to your schedule is like any new habit. If you've been flying by the seat of your pants for most your life, give yourself some time to adjust to this new discipline. There will be mistakes. But the more you can commit yourself to structuring your time every day with this calendar practice, the more likely it is that you'll begin to notice the effect it has on your life. You'll find yourself spending more time on the *doing,* and less on the negotiations with yourself on *whether* or *when* to do. Eventually, you'll come to see the time slotted for a non-favorite activity as a commitment that gets you to the fun thing that's on the schedule afterward.

As that famous sportswear company says: *Just do it.*

Between discussing calendars and goal-setting, this is a perfect time to talk about the single most important business book I have ever read: The Kaizen Way, by Robert Maurer. The subtitle of this book says it all: One Small Step Can Change Your Life.

This premise has proven true to me over and over whether working on my own business, or when helping other agents reach a much higher level of success in their business. The biggest goals in the world can be broken down into small steps that can be accomplished a little at a time, through a disciplined approach followed every day.

I'll illustrate this theory with a relatively simple example, using some metrics that will be explained in more detail in the next chapter. Let's say you want to grow your present real estate business by $200,000 a year. We'll assume that you profit, on average, $5,000 per client. That means you need to gain 40 more clients this year to grow your business by $200,000.

This seems like an incredible and daunting goal, doesn't it? So, I'd suggest you stop looking at that huge goal, and start looking at the small things you can do to eventually reach that goal.

You need 40 more clients, and you know that you get one client from every ten phone calls you make to past clients, friends, and family. That's 400 phone calls a year. Still seems a bit much. But let's say you only call people 44 weeks a year, which means that you make no phone calls to gain new clients for a full eight weeks a year – that's two months off! Now, we're down to making nine phone calls a week. Let's say you only make calls to gain new clients four days out of every week – that's three days off a week! Now, we're down to two-and-one-fourth phone calls every day. So, you make two phone calls for three days, and then you make three phone calls on the fourth day.

Come on now, you can make two or three phone calls a day for four days a week for 44 weeks a year, can't you? What do you think would happen if you were to walk up to anyone on the street and say "hey, would you make two phone calls for three days and then three phone calls on the fourth day for the next 44 weeks if I pay you $200,000?" I think most people would act like they had just won the lottery. Big, huge goals, broken down into small, doable steps—that's The Kaizen Way.

The level of change needed to take your business from dull and average to exciting and extraordinary is actually very small. Visualize a stereo tuner with a big volume knob that goes from 1 to 20. Most agents feel they need to crank the volume from 7 to 20 to change their business. That's monumental. In reality, when we analyze what agents currently do in their business, they're probably really at an 11 already. Just nudging their daily activity up to a 13 could be all it takes to reach their goals. 11 up to 13. Small steps. You can do this.

The Kaizen method helps many couch potatoes become marathon runners. You start running one day, and you get winded before you reach the mailbox. You reach the mailbox the next day and it's slightly easier. After a week, you can make it to the end of the block. After a month of daily running you can complete a mile. After two months, you're completing two miles. Slowly but surely, you gain ground every day. It might be an inch a day, but every day you gain.

Eventually, you build up to a 5K, then a 10K. After a year of consistent running, you can complete a half marathon. Then, after another year of training, you can complete the full marathon. You have trained your mind and body, over a long and difficult time period, to accomplish something great. Your success is not measured in the marathon, but in the inches you added to your run every single day.

The marathon analogy is apt for real estate agents. The bottom line is that if you can complete a 5K run, you can complete a marathon. If there is some physical ailment or impediment that makes it impossible to finish the 5K, then it may be impossible for you to finish a marathon. In real estate, if you can sell five homes a year and/or make $50,000 in commissions, you can reach whatever level of success you choose to reach in your real estate career. You have shown the basic aptitude for this business, and now it is simply the daily application of your business plan that can take you to wherever you wish to go.

Chapter Five: Set Your Goals, Achieve your Goals

Goal-Setting

One of the fundamental principles for success in your real estate business is that to achieve your idea of success, you have to identify what that is. In other words, to get *there,* you need to know where you're going; you have to **set a goal**. While this may sound ridiculously rudimentary, you would be surprised how many people have a general idea they are striving toward, but have not actually articulated precisely what they want. Is it any wonder, then, they have not attained it?

If you have not done so already, stop right now and decide your goal for your real estate business for the next 12 months, or your next fiscal year. How much money do you want to make? You can state this in terms of gross commission income, total sales revenue, or net income post-expenses and taxes. This number should be big—sufficiently big that it actually makes you gasp a little. More than you *need,* and definitely more than you're currently making.

Your goal should represent a reach, something you would feel very accomplished in attaining—but also not *so* out there that you can't really believe in it. Keep it within the realm of achievable. This involves knowing not only where you want to go, but where you currently *are*. Is this your first year in the business? You probably have a lot to learn, and your goals might encompass certain benchmarks about your professional development, as well as a more modest earnings target (for now). Do you already have things set up well, with a large sphere of referrals coming in from your database? If so, you may be in position to tweak your process of converting contacts into clients, such that a very large income increase is realistically within reach over the next 12 months. You are in the best position to know what a great goal is for you.

Got that number? OK, *write it down*. Display it proudly, where you'll see it all the time. It's like putting up a poster of the beach in Tahiti where you'd like to vacation, as a constant reminder. If you look at your number every single day, and post it in a spot where others see it too, you make it real, and you cement in your mind where you're headed this year.

Make Your Plan to Get There

Calculate Your Goal Transactions

Now that you've set your specific and quantified goal for the year, you need to work backward from that number to come up with your detailed plan—your personalized ***metrics***—that describes how you're going to get there.

The fundamental strategy in all real estate transactions involves a process of conversion: from a lead to a contact, to an appointment, to a sale. Think of the flow this way:

Leads → Contacts → Appointments → Sales

In the above formula, the strategy is in the *arrows*, which represent the actions you take as you move along the continuum to a completed transaction. The more you can quantify the amount of effort you need to put in to complete this conversion process, as well as *how many* completed conversions you need in a year, the more precisely you will be able to construct a plan on which you can rely to reach your goal.

Let's start by calculating the number of transactions you will need to complete, also known as your **goal transactions**. First, translate your articulated goal (the number you wrote down and now have framed above your computer) into a number stated as **gross commission income (GCI).** This is the amount of income that comes to you prior to expenses and taxes being taken out, so if your posted number reflects your actual take-home pay goal, add those amounts back in to arrive at your GCI.

Next, look back at the previous 12 months. Add up all your commissions for the year, and divide by the total number of commissions you received, to calculate your average **commission per transaction (CPT).**

Total Commission Income ÷ Number of Commissions = Commission perTransaction (CPT)

Now, divide your gross commission income (GCI) by your commission per transaction (CPT), to arrive at your **goal transactions (GT).** This is the number of transactions you will need to complete in order to meet your commissions goal.

Gross Commission Income ÷ Commission per Transaction = Goal Transactions GCI ÷ CPT = GT

Example:

You want to take home $150,000 after expenses and taxes. Assume taxes and expenses constitute approximately 40 percent of gross commissions, which would be an additional $100,000.

$150,000 + $100,000 = $250,000 Thus, your **GCI** would be $250,000

Over the previous 12 months, you earned $200,000 in total commissions, and you had 40 commissions for the year.

$200,000 ÷ 40 = $5,000 is your average commission Your **CPT** would be $5,000

Divide your goal GCI by your previous CPT to arrive at your number of goal transactions (GT).

$250,000 (GCI) ÷ $5,000 (CPT) = 50 (GT) Your **GT** would be 50

> “ **This means you need to close on 50 transactions at your average commission rate of $5,000 in order to make your desired take-home income of $150,000.** ”

In all my years of helping agents write and execute their business plans, this is the spot where most got tripped up. The vast majority of agents I met with were doing the right things, they just were not doing them enough!

This is why quantification of your business is so important. A great agent might be calling for an hour or two a week. After running their numbers in this way, we'd discover that they should really be calling for an hour and a half a day for four days a week. It really was not that dramatic of a shift in effort, but it could equal as much as a $100,000 increase in yearly GCI.

Quantify Your Goal, Part 1
Determining your Substantive Contacts Number

Now that you know how many transactions you have in your sights (your GT), you'll need to figure out what, exactly, you need to do to achieve this number.

Start by figuring out your necessary **qualified leads (QL).** I'm fond of saying that the definition of a qualified lead is just a "really, really good lead." Another definition of a qualified lead is any consumer who has expressed a real estate need, and has chosen you to fulfill that need. This ranges from a weak qualified lead, like someone getting your number from a For-Sale sign (they had a need for more information and called you), to a strong qualified lead, such as a past customer calling to have you give them a CMA on their house. Multiply your number of goal transactions **(GT)** by the number **2.4** to arrive at the number of qualified leads you will need in one year.

Goal Transactions x 2.4 = Qualified Leads Needed GT x 2.4 = QL

Next, calculate how many substantive contacts you'll need to reach this number of qualified leads. A substantive contact is a contact that moves a relationship forward in both quality and quantity of referrals received (see Chapter 6). In general, it takes an average of 17.2 substantive contacts to equal one qualified lead. So multiply your number of qualified leads needed in one year (QL) by the number 17.2 to get the total number of **substantive contacts** (SUBCONs) you need in one year.

Total Qualified Leads x 17.2 = Substantive Contacts per Year QL x 17.2 = SUBCONs/YEAR

Why 2.4 Qualified Leads per Goal Transaction and why 17.2 Substantive Contacts per Qualified Lead? Because we said so, that's why! In all seriousness, these numbers have held true as averages throughout our years and years of conducting training exercises and coaching agents. Of course, you must keep track of your own rates of return as you go forward. Perhaps after a full year of using these numbers, you determine that your averages are a bit different. At that point, you can use your collected data to make informed adjustments to these formulas in order to better describe your performance.

Break it down

Now, let's break that down even further. It's all well and good to say you need to talk to 2,000 people over the course of a year to reach your sales goal, but you need to put that into daily numbers in order to meaningfully transform your goal into a task list.

Take your total number of **yearly substantive contacts** (YEARLY SUBCONs), and divide that by 48 weeks. This presumes that there will be four weeks every year that you do not prospect. This will get you to the number of substantive contacts you need to make **every week** (WEEKLY SUBCONs) in order to reach your goal.

YEARLY SUBCONs ÷ 48 = WEEKLY SUBCONs

Now, take your number of WEEKLY SUBCONs and divide by four, to arrive at the number of substantive contacts you will need to make **each day** (DAILY SUBCONs), four days per week, 48 weeks per year. This presumes that there will be three full days each week that you do not prospect.

WEEKLY SUBCONs ÷ 4 = DAILY SUBCONs

This final calculation, your daily substantive contacts, is what we call ***your number.*** Etch this number into your brain for the year, as it represents the key stepping-stone to achieving your yearly income goal. Four days per week, 48 weeks per year, you will need to make this many substantive contacts with people in your database, in order to convert these contacts into your target number of transactions.

DAILY SUBCONs = **YOUR NUMBER**

Example:

Let's go back to the above goals. To make $150,000 in take-home income, you need a GT of 50 (50 closed transactions).

50 x 2.4 = 120	Your QL is 120

You will need 120 qualified leads per year.

120 x 17.2 = 2,064	Your YEARLY SUBCONs is 2,064

You will need to make 2,064 substantive contacts per year.

2,064 ÷ 48 = 43	Your WEEKLY SUBCONs is 43

You will need to make 43 substantive contacts per week (with 4 weeks off per year).

43 ÷ 4 = 10.75	Your DAILY SUBCONs is 10.75

You will need to make 10.75 substantive contacts per day (4 days per week).

Your NUMBER is 10.75

OK, got my number! Now what do I do?

Now that you have your number, it's time to set your strategy in place for making that number of substantive contacts each and every day of your plan for the year. The beauty of our system is that if you have recalibrated your mindset to appreciate the longer view, you really don't need to worry over every transaction, or about the amount of time in between each one. You can trust the numbers, and know that if you truly bring your 'A' game and make your required number of substantive contacts, you *will* get the results you have set as your goal.

It's time to establish your plan. Your specific course of action (your ***Methods***) will be something you determine after reading Section III of this book. But to start, you should look at your database of relationships, and break this list down into three categories (take a look at Chapter 6 for more detail):

➪	As	People you contact monthly
➪	Bs	People you contact quarterly
➪	Cs	People you contact every six months

Going back to our example, let's assume:

+	32 A's	32 x 12 =	384 SUBCONs
+	72 B's	72 x 4 =	288 SUBCONs
+	96 C's	96 x 2 =	192 SUBCONs
TOTAL:		864 YEARLY SUBCONS	

Using this strategy, you will have 864 of your 2,064 yearly substantive contacts from the categories in your current database.

2,064 - 864 = 1,200

You'll need to employ additional methods to make the remaining 1,200 substantive contacts per year in order to reach your goal.

Quantify Your Goal, Part 2 Calculating your Success Rate

You now know how many substantive contacts you need to make in order to achieve your annual goal. But let's break this down even further in order to refine exactly *how much of each type* of effort you'll need to undertake.

Not all forms of marketing or prospecting yield the same results. This is where keeping close watch on your own success rates[1] will help you to determine exactly what amount of effort is required for each transaction.

We have observed some general principles with respect to rates of return. Some agents like to use the standard of 40 contacts per sale as a universal multiplier to calculate their total contacts needed, and we agree that this can be a useful general rule of thumb.

However, not every type of contact has the same

1 Many people in the industry use the phrase "conversion rate" to refer to the number of contacts relative to a sale. However, the word "conversion" is also used to describe each point of movement along the continuum from lead to contact to appointment to sale. For the sake of clarity, we use the phrase "success rate" in this book to refer only to those contacts resulting in a sale.

weight. For example, when you're following up on an internet lead, a geo-farm response, or a sign call, you must factor in the need to build better rapport with that contact. These are not people who already know, like and trust you, and so you will not be able to convert nearly as many of these contacts as you would from your sphere of influence.

Put another way, your success rate is partly dependent upon where your contacts fall along the Trust Curve:

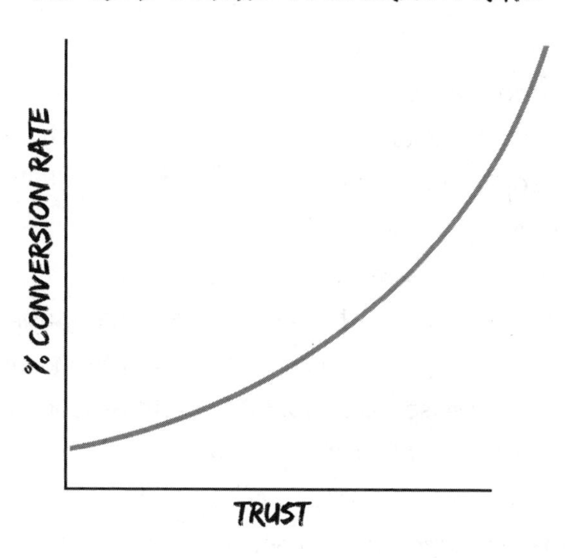

The higher the level of trust someone has in you, the more likely it is you will complete a transaction with them. You will have a higher success rate with people from your sphere, who fall higher on the Trust Curve; you will have a lower success rate for people you don't know as well, who fall lower on the Trust Curve.

What this means, in terms of your contact metrics, is that you will need to make *more* contacts with people you don't know than you would with people in your sphere in order to achieve the same number of transactions. You will have a *lower* success rate. Thus, when you think about your marketing strategies, you'll want to factor in your *actual* success rate, as experienced with each approach.

Let's have some more math!

Refer back to your GCI, your **gross commission income,** which you used in the previous formulas. We can break that down by market strategy, multiplying the number of leads by the success rate you have experienced for that type of contact. This will give you the number of contacts needed for each type of lead or market strategy. Then, you add together all these categorical components to arrive at your GCI.

Starting with your sphere of influence (**SOI**), given that typically people move every 7-10 years, about 10 percent of the people you know will need your services each year. If you've done your job staying in contact and top of mind, you should expect to get their business. Take a moment right now to check: add up the number of people in your sphere of influence database, and look at your transactions from last year. Does this track, at least approximately, with the 10 percent figure? If not, you probably need to give some attention to your database management practices (see Chapter 6).

If you have 200 people in your sphere, this should produce 20 transactions per year. This may be stated as:

Sphere of Influence ÷ 10 = Transactions from Sphere per Year SOI ÷ 10

To calculate the amount of commission income you will receive from this portion of your business, multiply this figure by your

CPT (**commission per transaction):**

Sphere of Influence ÷ 10 x Commission per Transaction = Gross Commission Income from Sphere SOI ÷ 10 x CPT = GCI_{SOI}

Example:

200 ÷ 10 x \$5,000 = \$100,000

If this number isn't greater than your targeted goal GCI, you'll need to supplement with other lead sources to increase your overall GCI, and continue to add more contacts to your database.

To determine your *success rate* with each additional source of business, you can look at the quantity of leads, divided by number of transactions generated by that particular marketing effort.

Number of Leads from Strategy ÷ Number of Transactions from Strategy = Success Rate of Strategy

To determine the GCI of any given marketing effort, multiply the number of leads by your success rate and your Commission per Transaction.

Number of Leads from Strategy **x** Success Rate of Strategy **x** Commission per Transaction = Gross Commission Income from Strategy

Let's say you generated 300 internet leads,[2] and three resulted in a sale. Your success rate with your internet leads strategy is 1 percent.

$$GCI_{internet} = \text{Number of internet Leads} \times \text{internet Success Rate} \times CPT$$

Example:

$$GCI_{internet} = 300 \times 1\% \times \$5{,}000 = \$15{,}000$$

Keeping Track of your Data

At this point, you may be wondering where all these numbers are coming from. To really know how you're doing (and to be able to project with reliability how you're going to perform), the numbers need to come from *you*. It's important to keep records of your marketing efforts and where your leads are coming from. Keep track of everything you do, every day. That way, you can make educated business decisions. We recommend that you review your numbers monthly, quarterly and annually.

---

2 For more on how to approach and plan internet leads and best practices, see Chapter 8. For the moment, we reference this strategy for purposes of demonstrating how you calculate a success rate specific to a particular marketing method, of which you may have several.

Extra Credit: Effect of Additional Variables on Success Rate

You may feel that you now have enough of an overview of your plan to be comfortable calculating projections for your business. However, there are some further refinements you may want to make, based on additional variables that will affect your success rate.

Response Rate

Your response rate is the number of inquiries from a particular marketing effort, divided by the number of people targeted.

Number of Inquiries from Effort ÷ Number of People Targeted = Response Rate

Example #1:

Number of calls ÷ Number of post cards mailed 3 phone calls ÷ 2,000 postcards = 0.15%

Example #2:

Number of website registers ÷ Number of views 10 new inquiries ÷ 200 page views = 5%

Conversion Rate

Your conversion rate is the rate at which you're able to successfully convert a lead to an appointment, and an appointment into a sale. Depending on how in-depth you want to go, you can look at your appointment conversion rate and appointment-to-closed-sales ratio separately.

Appointment Conversion Rate = # of contracts ÷ # of appointments (Both Buyer & Seller)

Listing-to-Sale Ratio = # of Homes Sold ÷ # of Homes Listed

Buyer Closed-Sale Ratio = # of Homes Sold ÷ # of Buyers

For now we'll just combine them into a simple conversion rate. Example:

1 sale ÷ 100 internet leads = 1%

If you converted 1 in 100 internet leads that would be a 1 percent conversion rate.

Success Rate

Success Rate = Response Rate x Conversion Rate

From our previous Example #2, if you captured 5 percent of the visitors to your website, and turned 1 percent of them into sales your overall success rate for website traffic or pay-per-click ads would be 0.05 percent.

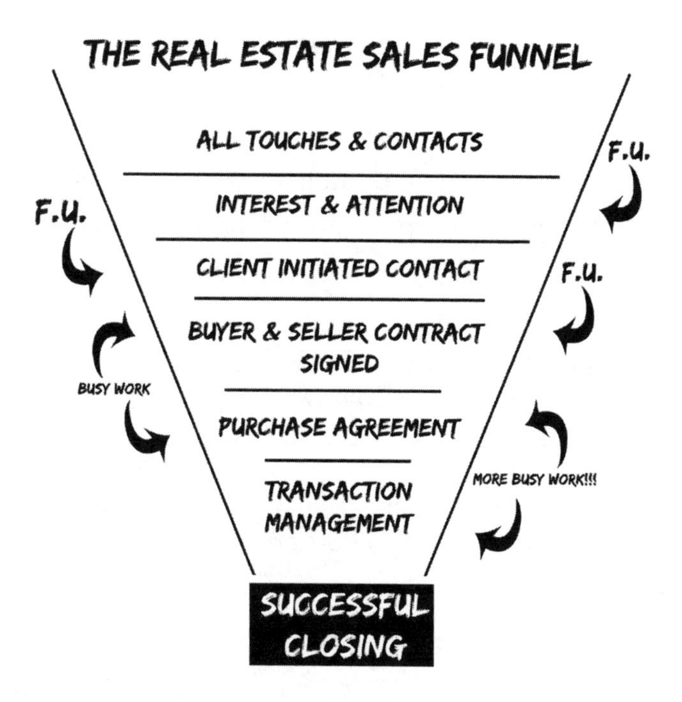

By looking backwards at your success rate for each source of business, you can make better decisions for the following year. This will help you determine the number of actions need per each marketing effort required to hit your goal. We recommend starting with your sphere of influence, and only adding one or two additional sources of business at a time. Mastering a source of prospecting and increasing your success rate has far more of an impact than attempting to do a little of everything.

Analyzing your Return on Investment

You've only got a finite amount of time, and certainly a finite budget. Thus there are limitations on the scalability of your marketing efforts. Just because you were able to convert 1 percent of your internet leads doesn't mean you can just generate ten times more leads, and make ten times more money. Eventually, the cost of generating those leads would exceed your budget, and you would not have the time to follow up with each person.

For this reason it's important to consider your return on investment, both in terms of the financial cost of marketing, and also your time devoted to prospecting and follow-up.

Return on Investment = (Gross Commission – Cost of Marketing) ÷ Cost of Marketing

Looking backward, if you spent $4,500 to generate the leads above, and made $15,000 on the sales, your return on investment would be a multiple of 2.3.

Example: ($15,000 - $4,500) ÷ $4,500

Wow! You've more than tripled your money. But wait. How much time was spent following up with the 297 other people who didn't buy?

The answer will be different for everyone, but the lesson is never discount your time!

You need to know how much commission you have made in the past, including how much effort and money went into each successful transaction, to be able to realistically calculate what you *are able to* make. To grow your business and increase your income, you can calculate how much more you'll need to invest in order to arrive at your desired GCI.

Cost of Sale

To make future projections, we look at the cost of sale.

Cost of Sale = Total Cost of Marketing Effort ÷ Number of Sales Received

Once again, using our example:

Cost of Sale = $4,500 ÷3 = $1,500

Each of your three internet lead sales cost you $1,500.

Here we can see that it costs $1,500 to make a sale, so any marketing expenditure less than that may not consistently yield a return. If you're not at a stage where you're comfortable with the minimum cost of sale, simply don't use that method (at least for now).

Cost per Lead

We can also derive the ***cost per lead*** of each marketing effort.

Cost Per Lead = Total Cost of Marketing ÷ # of Leads Received

Example:

Cost per lead = $4,500 ÷ 300 = $15

Decreasing your cost per lead, or increasing your conversion rate, will help you reduce your cost of sale and increase your return on investment.

Marketing beyond your sphere of influence in any category is not worth doing unless you're able to consistently dedicate the time and money required. Marketing dollars should be allocated based on a proven ROI, until the point of saturation. Eventually, another dollar in will not yield another dollar out, and just as there was a minimum, so there is also a maximum amount of business achievable.

Keep in mind that each market performs differently. However, these equations can be applied universally, by inputting your own variables. These formulas are provided to help you understand the metrics behind your marketing. In order to master the art of marketing, you must look at each variable independently, and understand its impact on results.

Realtor.com provides a handy calculator for their leads. You can substitute your numbers from any lead source to get the same results: http://marketing.realtor.com/roi/12months

PART III

Methods

GROWING YOUR WORLD OF REFERRALS, LEADS AND CONTACTS

Chapter 6: Database Management: How to track and 'touch' your Sphere

Creating and Maximizing your Database

As we've mentioned, the best place to start enhancing and growing your contacts is in your sphere of influence. We will refer to this as your database. Think of your database as a list of relationships. It is the lifeblood of your business. There is no technology or information that is more important than your database.

An important distinction must be drawn between your *database* and a *mailing list*. A mailing list is simply a way to get leads from people who live in a common geographic area, have signed up for more information on your website, attended an event at which your presented, etc. Your **database,** on the other hand, is a **list of *relationships*** which**,** properly cultivated and nurtured, **can sustain and grow your business** for decades to come.

Think of your database as an engine, the contacts are the cogs and sprockets that make your engine produce its output: closed transactions. The fuel that makes the engine run is *substantive contacts.* When your engine is running at maximum efficiency, you will know exactly how much fuel to add in order to receive the desired amount of output.

The "Nicollet Mall Test"

The people who make up your database are essential to your successful business. The quality of your database content can mean the difference between languishing at a subsistence level of production for years, and achieving great levels of success while truly enjoying your clients.

Who should go into your database? Basically, people you know and like.

In downtown Minneapolis, where we're from, there is a pedestrian walkway called the Nicollet Mall. (For those of you not familiar with the Twin Cities, you might know the Nicollet Mall as the place where Mary Tyler Moore threw her hat up in the air at the beginning of The Mary Tyler Moore Show in the mid-1970s.) Like most pedestrian walkways that run through downtown areas, Nicollet Mall is home to a collection of business people, homeless people, young, old, rich, poor, homeowners, renters, and the occasional real estate agent.

In preparing my database, I used Nicollet Mall as a litmus test. In a clean notebook, I wrote down the names of every single person I knew in the world.

Creating my original database took weeks and weeks. I'd write down a hundred names, and then, days later, remember one of my best friends I had accidentally omitted. It helped a little bit to think by context. For instance, I'd think of everyone

I knew from high school (including teachers and staff), then everyone I knew from college, then everyone I knew from church, then everyone I knew from my kid's school, etc. I'd write and write these names for pages upon pages.

There was one test that every name had to pass before being added to the notebook. I'd imagine myself walking north on Nicollet Mall, while the person whose name had just popped into my head was walking south. If we saw each other, liked and knew each other well enough to come to the middle of the Mall and talk, they would be added, if not they wouldn't be included. For example if I looked across the Mall and saw Jeff Olson from my church, and we came together to talk, then he went on the list. He might not be the closest relationship in my database, and it had yet to be determined how many referrals he could send my way, but he was familiar enough to me to be in the database. Because the purpose of the database is to build your business through connections and referrals, time and metrics would tell me how long he, or anyone, should remain there.

Once I felt I had a robust list, I started editing. Remember, your database is a list of relationships from which you want to foster connections and cultivate referrals. Fostering and cultivating takes time and energy. Thus, while you definitely want a healthy, sizeable database, you don't want to include people who won't yield the appropriate return for your investment of time and energy, regardless of how much you may like them.

This may seem a bit cut-throat, but it's not. You can maintain a list of friends or fellow agents with whom you socialize but who are not included in your database. The database is a machine. It has a business purpose. For the machine to run smoothly and efficiently, the fuel must be pure. Keep your database for business reasons only, and include those people who will return your time and energy with the highest number of referrals.

Here are some of the people I crossed of my database:

- **Competitive agents**. Don't get me wrong- there were a lot of real estate agents I kept in my database. However, most were elsewhere in the country, or at least on the other side of town, and might be referral sources. For purposes of my database (which I would mine for referrals), competitive agents in my working territory (even those on my friend list) were deleted.
- **Out-of-market contacts with no referral base**. I operated out of the Minneapolis/St. Paul area. If one of my good friends from church moved to Ohio, and they didn't stay in touch with people back in Minneapolis, I would most likely remove them from my database. At the very least, I would move them to a category with less frequent contact, keeping an eye on whether it made sense to take them off the list entirely. Again, this is a pure reflection of the number of referrals generated, relative to my time and energy.
- **Jerks**. This is actually a tough one, and one that I see agents struggling with all of the time. But seriously, cross them off the list. I don't care if a client is sending you a million-dollar referral every two days. If they don't respect you and what you do for a living, cut them from your database. Jerks refer jerks about 90 percent of the time. That's too high a risk to mess with. Drop all jerks from your database, and spend all of the time and energy that they would have taken (and they take up the most!) creating new database members

or making new contacts. You'll replace any missing referral numbers, and your life will be happier and healthier for booting the jerks out of your database.

Reticular Activating System

The Reticular Activating System a concept that was introduced to me by Brian Buffini. Please understand that I know very little about the science of the brain (I'm in the real estate business!). But this theory makes sense to me, and more importantly, has been hugely helpful to me. So, bear with me while I take a stab at neuroscience, and keep an open mind.

Your Reticular Activating System (RAS) is that little part of your brain that regulates your transitions between sleep and wakefulness, or conscious and unconscious. It also serves as the automatic mechanism inside your brain that brings relevant information to your attention.

Let's say you're walking through Target on an especially busy Sunday. Noises are all around you, from crying babies, groups of shopping teens, music over the intercom, squeaky shopping cart wheels. Suddenly, someone says your name from 20 feet away, at a normal voice level. Your RAS goes into high alert, distinguishing between all of the background noises in the store, and your very specific attention to one sound in particular.

Or, let's say it's time to buy a new car. You go out car shopping one day and you take a look at the new Volvo S60. You've never really noticed this car on the road before, and you're thinking over this major purchase. Now, as you drive around town, it seems that all you see are Volvo S60s! It's like *everyone* is driving one of these cars. In reality, you've been passing them for years, but they have always been blurred background images of which your mind took little notice. Now, your RAS is awakened every time it sees a Volvo S60.

How does the RAS come into play with your database? Every time you reach out to a database member, you are activating their RAS about you and the real estate market. Many agents scoff at the idea of contacting their sphere for recommendations because they say, "I don't feel comfortable begging my friends for referrals."

I can tell you that I have *never* begged anyone for a referral. At times, and only occasionally, I might add "Hey, if you know anyone who needs helps in real estate, have them give me a call," to the end of a conversation, and then I'd drop it. No overt requests for referrals. I'd simply pick up the phone and call a good friend and sphere group member. Usually, *they* would bring up the real estate subject by asking, "What's the market like right now?" or something of the sort. I'd answer, and then move the conversation back to them.

Countless times throughout the years, the person I was talking to would say, "Wait a second, I know someone who is looking for a house right now," or, "You know what? My neighbor was just talking about moving." All I did was help them activate their own RAS. From background noise to consciousness.

Moreover, I'd often get a call from the sphere group member within a day or two after our interaction. The RAS remains in a state of activation for a few days. A week or more after that, someone might come up to my sphere group member and say, "Hey, I need to sell my house," but they wouldn't remember me. At some point, I go back into being background noise, until we have another interaction.

Requesting a Referral

The RAS is the reason that the very best time to ask for a referral is while you're actively working with a buyer or seller. When a couple is looking to buy their first house together, their RAS is stimulated for this activity. When this couple goes to work, or church, or out with friends, guess what they always see? Other couples looking to buy their first home!

They talk about it, and go to message boards about it, and watch television shows about it. It consumes their life. I hear young home-buying couples say all the time, "it seems like everybody is looking to buy right now," because that is all they see when their RAS is on high alert.

Most agents wait to ask for a referral, if they ask at all, until they are sitting at the closing table, or maybe soon thereafter. Guess what young couples who have just bought their first home see all over the place? Other young couples who have *just bought* their first home.

It happens all the time. Suddenly, their life switches from chat rooms and television shows about buying a home, to chat rooms and television shows about how to fix up, remodel or furnish their first home. You've missed your chance to take advantage of their RAS at the perfect moment!

And, **YES**, you do have to ask for a referral! Ask all the time so that you become used to the rhythm and timing of asking for a referral. Asking someone for a referral is a lot like telling a good joke. Too soon, it can seem pushy, and too late, it can seem forced. It's best to listen closely as you're showing a home to buyers. Sometimes, they'd say something like "Cliff and Ellen should see this one." I'd chime in with "well, I'd love to show it to them, if you don't have any interest." Two purposes were accomplished by this interaction: I gauged their level of interest, and at the same time, opened the door to the idea of them providing me referrals.

The best time to ask a *seller* for referrals is at the meeting in which you are signing the listing contract. A sentence like "I'm sure you know a lot of other people that are looking to sell, I'd love it if you passed along my name and number." Gauge the level of response to determine whether you should push the subject.

The bottom line is to strike while the RAS is hot. Ask for referrals from your buyers and sellers when all the world is buyers and sellers to them.

Goal Achieving Tool

Your reticular activating system is like a filter between your conscious mind and your subconscious mind. It takes instructions from your conscious mind and passes them on to your subconscious. For example, the instruction might be "listen for anyone saying my name."

There are some interesting points about your RAS that make it an essential tool for achieving goals. First, you can deliberately program the reticular activating system by choosing the exact messages you send from your conscious mind. For example, you can set goals, or say affirmations, or visualize your objectives. Of course, if we keep thinking that we can't achieve a goal, our subconscious will help us *not* achieve it.

Second, your reticular activating system cannot tell if what it's experiencing is real, or purposely created. In other words, it tends to believe whatever message you give it. Imagine that you're going to be giving a speech. You can practice giving that

speech by visualizing it in your mind. This 'pretend' practice should improve your ability to give the speech.
It's so important for real estate agents to practice their listing and buyer presentations before they are given. Practice in front of a mirror, or record the practice session on your phone and then play it back. Yes, it may be painful, but practice is extremely important in any sort of presentation. Your business rests upon your ability to successfully present (whether it be an offer, a listing presentation, or a buyer presentation), so practice often.

Substantive Contacts

I'm pretty sure I never uttered the word *substantive* until I was in real estate. What is a substantive contact? It's a contact (or a touch, a communication, etc.) that actually does something. As they say in the public relations business, a substantive contact "moves the needle." It moves a referral relationship forward in both quality and quantity of referrals received.

Not just any contact is substantive, though. In a world filled with more and more noise, only a few forms of communication really cut through the din and are perceived as genuine.

I get a lot of pushback from agents on what kind of contact they believe is, and is not, substantive. You can add or subtract from this list as you see fit, but do so with extreme caution. Here is a little litmus test for you: How would you choose to propose, or be proposed, marriage? How would you prefer to find out that you just got fired, or that someone was breaking up with you? Via text? Via email? Either would seem a little impersonal and callous, wouldn't it? So, why do we feel that our greatest business asset - the relationships that we have with our sphere - are just fine being left to some email drip campaign or a group text?

If you want to grow your business, have real and substantive contacts with your sphere group members. It will expand your friendships *and* will get you an amazing number of referrals.

The Three Best Substantive Contact Methods:

1. The in-person meeting

This is the absolute gold standard in substantive contacts. No other contact method beats meeting face-to-face. Any in-person meeting counts as a substantive contact. This could even be a listing or a buyer appointment. Remember, the best time to ask directly for a referral is when you are actively in the process of working with someone.

In an effort to maximize your number of in-person meetings, have at least three business lunches or dinners per week with sphere group members. Ways to mix this up include:

- Business Breakfast

  The ***business breakfast*** gets you out and dressed for work early in the morning, and both you and your sphere group member are fresh and undistracted by the events of day. Further, you have an easy excuse to get going and not drag out the meeting: "Well, we should be getting to work."

  At a breakfast meeting, it's natural to talk about work, as you are both heading there soon. Talk of work allows you to show off what you have going on right now, and how you're helping people. For instance, if you want to sell your sphere group member on buying some investment real estate, it would be helpful to say

"Today, I'm taking out a gentleman looking to diversify his investment portfolio by purchasing a multi-family property." Not a direct solicitation, but it reminds your sphere group member that this is a service you provide.

- Large Client Gathering

Another great way to have in-person meetings with your sphere group members is through a ***client gathering***. Some successful agents host large holiday parties or summer boat rides. These type of events can cost a lot of money, but bring together your entire sphere. When your sphere group gathers in large numbers based on your invitation, you can bet that you (and what a great real estate agent you are) will be the hot topic of conversation. This is a great opportunity to mix your As, Bs, and Cs--in other words, your raving fans with your lukewarm fans. The blend will make some As into A+s, Bs into As, and Cs into Bs.

Client Party Ideas:

- Wine & cheese parties
- Bowling day
- Restaurant deals
- Boat rides
- Yearly parties
- Holiday parties
- Make-overs
- Beer brewing
- Sporting events

- Individual Monthly Deal

Big client parties, as noted, can be costly. The good news is, you can start small. Think about a ***favorite restaurant***

or bar in an area that is geographically accessible to a large number of your sphere group members. Approach the owner or manager and say,

> **"Hi, my name is ________, and I'm a real estate agent in the area. I run a program that rewards my friends, family and past clients for referring me business. Every month, I email my entire list and let them know of a special deal that I'm offering exclusively to them, as a thank you for their support. If someone I refer this way comes in on a Tuesday night [or choose a night that is particularly slow for this establishment] and says that they're a part of my customer appreciation program, is it possible to give them some sort of deal?"**

These deals could be half off of a second entrée, a free drink with a meal, free dessert, etc. Sometimes, it's difficult to get these deals for free from the restaurant, so you might say:

> **"I understand, but would you offer everyone who says they are a member of my Client Appreciation Program a free appetizer or dessert, and then pay for them with my credit card?"**

The fact is, very few of your sphere group members will take advantage of this offer, so this probably won't cost you much money. But making the offer gives you a chance to call several members of your database personally and send out an email to everyone, providing an important contact every month.

Make sure you go to the restaurant on the designated day to see if any of your database members are there, so that you can make a person-to-person contact. Be sure to eat at a separate table so that they don't feel pressure to invite you to join, or to join you.

➪ "Pop-By"

While on the subject of person-to-person contacts, it's a good time to talk about the ***Pop-By***. This is a term coined by Brian Buffini and it refers to the practice of making an unannounced visit to a client, to bring them a small gift or item of value. Buffini talks about dropping by with a gardening trowel in the spring, or a ketchup-mustard-relish basket around the Fourth of July (with a note saying, "Just popping-by to Ketchup and let you know I Relish your referrals. From your real estate agent who really cuts the Mustard.") This may sound a bit hokey, but the bottom line is that it works.

To create an effective pop-by, remember that the primary purpose is to deepen your relationship with your best clients. The gift you give is a token of your appreciation. Use your creativity to bring thoughtful or useful gifts to your clients. The true value of a pop-by is that you demonstrate care through the investment of your time and individualized attention. Keep it short and sweet, and start with your favorite people. Be genuine in your appreciation, as well as in your excitement about your business.

↳ "Reverse Pop-By"

I have received many good quality referrals from pop-bys. But they can be somewhat intimidating. And, yes, I have barged in on more than one moment that left me embarrassed, and might have even hurt a client relationship.

So, I started something I call the ***reverse pop-by***. I wouldn't drop by with a gift unannounced, but I would drop by, announced, to pick something up. During the late-90s and early 2000s I had a good business working with new doctors at the University of Minnesota who were relocating to the area. Through this association, I became very active with the Ronald McDonald House at the University.

Once a month, I would call 5 percent of my database members (about 15 people) and say, "Hey, I would like to drop by this Thursday night and pick up something for my favorite charity, the Ronald McDonald House. They don't need food, but they need dry goods. If I drop by, can I pick up some toilet paper, or paper towels?" Tell them exactly what you want to pick up, and let them know they shouldn't go out and buy anything (they usually do, though) because you just want them to contribute any extra products they might have around the house. When that particular Thursday night rolls around, you get to go to each of the houses you called and pick up the requested items. People feel more open and less put-off when they are giving you something, rather than the other way around. And invariably, clients will want to talk about their house and the real estate business, and it becomes a perfect chance for a person-to-person contact.

2. The person-to-person phone call

Pick up your phone, and call people. Seems simple. For some reason, this easy act induces a level of terror in some people that affects their central nervous system, to the point where they cannot pick up a piece of plastic, dial a few numbers, and speak.

Your phone is one of the most incredible communication devices ever invented. It fundamentally changed the geo-political landscape; it changed the world's economic system. Larger and far more intimidating causes have been undertaken with a phone call than you calling a past client to see how their child is enjoying the 8th grade, right?

The terror of making a phone call is very common, though. It has been closely linked to the fear of rejection. We have little to no problem calling someone who we already know likes us. But if it's been a while, or if we have lingering doubts about how the person on the other end of the line perceives us, calling someone on the phone presents the possibility of rejection.

Psychologists have linked the fear of rejection to that of death, since rejection makes us question our worth and thus our very reason to exist. This is the same root fear that manifests in those who are afraid of public speaking. So, if you get nervous about making calls, consider yourself in good company.

OK, so it's terrifying. Now get over it. The best way to get past the fear of making phone calls is to make phone calls. Every day. Habitualize making phone calls, and it will become easier.

When tallying a phone call as a substantive contact, leaving someone a *voicemail does not count*. You may be thinking: "I hardly ever get someone on the phone these days." But for best results, try to call someone two times, and don't leave a message. On the third try, if they aren't there, leave a message. Perhaps share in your voicemail that "you have tried a few times" to get a hold of them. Count it as a half of a contact that will be made into a whole contact *if* they call back and you talk person-to-person.

Leaving a message is a nice way of saying, "I was thinking of you," which is a nice way of bettering a relationship. Therefore, it does not have *zero* worth. It just does not have as much as an actual person-to-person phone call.

3. Hand-Written Note

Do not discount this one, because no single activity in my life has earned me more money than writing hand-written notes.

There are few better ways to efficiently build a relationship. I say "efficiently," because you can write five notes in a half-hour, but you can't have five substantive phone calls in that time, and you certainly can't have five substantive person-to-person meetings in that amount of time. Hand-written notes can even be completed between 5:00 and 5:30 a.m., when phone calls or person-to-person meetings usually involve something different (and usually less pleasant) than discussing real estate referrals.

Make your hand-written notes short, but meaningful. A couple of sentences in length is fine. Reference something in your shared past with the recipient, or something that came up in your last phone call or person-to-person meeting. Make it real and genuine.

I wrote five hand-written notes every single day for seven solid years. I wrote my five notes on my birthday, on the days my kids were born, on the day my dad died, when I was suffering from Lyme's Disease, every single day for seven years. The only thing that stopped me after seven years was transitioning from an agent to a broker. I continued to write notes, and I still do to this day, but in a slightly less regimented fashion.

A funny thing happens when you write five notes a day. At first, it's easy. You just go down your database, and send everyone a little reminder that you're thinking of them, and wishing them well. Then, you get through your database, and you start scratching your head about who to write to next.

That's when the beauty of hand-written notes starts really kicking in. You begin to go about your day looking for people to write to: the kid at the gas station, the barista at Starbucks, the lady that helped you at Kinko's. All of them deserve notes from you.

After a time, your notecards become half business-building, and half gratitude-giving. In a world where we're constantly peppered with bad news and stress, you find yourself moving through your days looking for all of the positive things that happen to you, and all of the great people you meet, because you know you have to write those damn notes tomorrow morning! When you look at life in this fashion, it starts seeming a bit brighter, and you see opportunities are around every corner.

Habitualize

Notice the habitualization of each of the above contact methods. They are all hard to do randomly. You can always find a reason *not* to make a phone call or write a hand-written note. But, if you set aside a certain time every day for these activities, and then follow your schedule religiously, you'll find that they become easy to do after a while.

You'll even get to a point when you think, *did I write my hand-written notes today?* And when you go back and check, sure enough. You did. But you've created such a habit that you don't even notice it.

The trick to building a habit is getting through the first one- to four-week period. When you start an activity like phone calling for an hour a day, or writing five hand-written notes per day, you are pumped for the first week. *You're going to rock this!* Then, the second week creeps in, with less energy and commitment and, of course, there is always something else to do, and some emergency that absorbs your attention. Stay at it. If you can get through weeks 2, 3 and 4, you'll most likely have made your activity into a habit.

Have you heard the old saying: *28 days to make a habit and five days to break it*? That's why I was so religious about writing my notes, because after going through the trouble of making my hard-won new habit, I was terrified of breaking it.

In order to make it through weeks 2, 3, and 4, it is best to set a plan, mark it in your calendar and follow it. Pre-write yourself encouraging sticky notes about *why* you're performing these activities, and put them on your mirror so that they face you every morning. Leave some in your calendar, and on your car dashboard. The messages should remind you of how your business and personal life can be transformed if you habituate these activities.

Another idea is to find an "accountability buddy" who is trying to build the same habits. Call each other every day. Send one another encouraging emails, and write each other supportive hand-written notes. An accountability buddy, as well as positive self-encouragement, can get you through weeks 2, 3, and 4.

Once you've made it through that first month, you can congratulate yourself on your great new habit! Sticking with it beyond this point will be like brushing your teeth—you wouldn't think of not doing it.

Tips:

- Always be seeking a reason for the next contact: *What should I talk to people about?*
- Instead of thinking of yourself as "bothering" friends and clients for referrals, consider that you are building real and lasting relationships.

Categorize Your Database

Anyone who has worked with a real estate coach should know about categorizing their database. We use the conventional A-B-C method, but with a few unique twists.

Categorizing your database will help you schedule your time, while ensuring that your emphasis and energy are directed to the proper places. If we fail to prioritize one type of database member over another, we fail to properly allocate our precious time and energy.

Having said that, know that this list is flexible and changeable. If someone is mistakenly put down as a C and they should be an A (or *vice versa*) your business will not come grinding to a halt, with bankruptcy on the horizon. This is a loose categorization that you can refine over time. As you refine, you become more efficient and effective.

The biggest mistake you can make with your database is to have too many people in it. I've met with agents who have 1,300 database members. That simply doesn't work. You can have 1,300 people on a mailing list, or on a newsletter email drip. But it is difficult, if not actually impossible, to maintain relationships with 1,300 people.

Keep the database short and honest. A concise database will increase your referrals by ensuring you grow your relationships through quality contacts and get many more referrals then you were receiving previously as a result. Most readers of this book could double, or even triple, their business immediately just by getting more referrals out of their database.

A's

An 'A' is a database member who will connect you to one closed transaction per year. It might be through a referral, or possibly it's the database member who buys or sells, or invests in real estate frequently. Either way, if I have 16 As on my list, that means I can absolutely take it to the bank that I will close 16 transactions a year because of them. If someone gives you one closed transaction every year, they are probably pretty close to you.

An A database member should receive a substantive contact once a month. That may seem like a lot, but you can work this into a routine over time. For instance, call an A member on the phone (person-to-person contact) and catch up. While on the phone, propose that you two should get together for lunch sometime soon. Suggest a date about a month away. Then, in a month, you have a nice lunch. Get up to speed on what your contact is doing, both at work and for fun. Catch up on the status of their family. Then, a little less than a month after the lunch, write a hand-written follow-up note that touches on a topic or two that you discussed. A month after that, follow up on the note. In this way, you're having a substantive contact once a month, and really growing a true relationship that will solidify the one closed transaction per year you receive from this person.

B's

A 'B' database member should bring one closed transaction to you about once every four years. Alternatively, one in every four B database members will bring you a closed transaction every year. Thus, if you have 40 B database members, you can count on ten closed transactions every year from them.

A B database member should receive a substantive contact from you once every quarter, or every three months.

C's

A 'C' database member should bring a closed transaction to you once every eight years on average. Or, one in every eight C database members will bring a closed transaction to you every year. Thus, if you have 80 C database members, then you can count on ten closed transactions every year from them.

A C database member should receive a substantive contact from you once every six months.

Please note that there is no D level. As Brian Buffini says: "D stands for delete."

Is this formula written in stone? Of course not. You can apply your own contact metrics after you've tracked your results over a long period of time. But you have to start with some protocol as to how often you get in touch with people, and how your database is categorized.

The beauty of categorizing your database this way, and habitualizing your frequency of contact, is that you are *creating* the success of your referrals by attending to the most productive relationships for your business. A C database member is not a C only because they have historically given you a closed transaction once every eight years. They're a C because you want to *ensure they stay* someone who gives you a closed transaction once every eight years. The frequency and sincerity of your contact can make a database member perform consistently with their level of categorization.

Why is this a great thing? Let's say you want to raise your average list price. Start with the premise that database members refer people similar to themselves. For instance, a database member that lives in a $300,000 home has an over 80 percent chance of referring someone who has, or is looking to buy, a $300,000 home. You know that As refer more often than Bs, and that Bs refer more often than Cs. You can also move database members up or down based on their performance. Move a C that lives in a $700,000 home up to the B level, and move a B that lives in a $210,000 home down to the C level. A C that owns a $150,000 home might be deleted from your database and placed on a mailing or email newsletter list.

However, it's best to never move a database member up more than one level at a time. The increase in contact might give them whiplash. By moving database members methodically, you can slowly raise your average list price over the course of time.

In a similar fashion, you can alter your database member categories when you change the area that you work. Move database members that are in your target area up a level in your categorization, and move database members down a level who are not in your target area. Over time, you can grow the exact business that you want. By effectively making use of your database and where you put your attention, you can target areas, types of clients, and price ranges.

Social Media

Social media may be the most discussed, yet most underutilized and misused tool in the real estate profession. Social media, at its core, allows us to be connected to our sphere. It collects (most of) your friends and family, from different times in your life, all in one place, accessible from your desk chair or wherever you and your smartphone are.

This makes social media, such as Facebook, a fantastic way to manage your social and family life. But what does that have to do with your real estate marketing? Here's the Big Secret: if you're connecting optimally with your sphere, they are the *same thing*. People do not want to be sold to. They want to believe that the people they connect with on Facebook are there for more genuine purposes. I absolutely believe—and have experienced—that coming from a place of contribution and caring generates legitimate relationships that result in additional transactions.

Keep in mind that social media is a living organism, and as such is susceptible to constant change. Within a few years, we may be looking at a completely different landscape of social technology, and it's important to stay abreast of the best ways to maintain authentic connection.

There are dozens of books and hundreds of websites dedicated to the topic of social media for real estate agents. There are even sites and services that (try to) do it for you. But this is not the task to outsource. We already know what it looks and feels like when automation overtakes certain forms of interpersonal exchange—think of trying to have a conversation with Siri, beyond asking a specific question. Siri can't be your friend. But in less than 30 minutes per day, you can have an insight into the lives of your potential customers, and connect with them in a way they'll remember. Why would you farm that out?

> "NOTE: Before you even get to social media, make sure your **website** is the professional presence you need. The details of your **website** are addressed more extensively in Chapter 8, but let this be a reminder of how all your marketing efforts ultimately intersect and feed each other. **Improving your real estate social media presence starts with your website**. Posting links on social channels that lead to badly designed or poorly optimized pages on your site will fail to get visitors to stay long enough to convert them into legitimate leads."

The Facebook Diet

As an approach regarding *how* to use Facebook, we recommend the "Facebook Diet." There are only three things you have to do. And like any diet, it's the consistency that matters, rather than the quantity of actions (i.e. number of messages or size of your sphere). Done properly, you can engage a wide audience in a very small amount of time. If you follow our formula, 15 to 30 minutes of Facebook time per day should create six to eight additional transactions per year for your business.

1. Be present.

Imagine social media to be like a coffee shop you go to every day, where inside are people that you know. Some days are good, some are bad; some days it's snowing, some days it's sunny. You interact with people about both the high and low things in life.

As in a coffee shop, on Facebook you may see someone and ask simply, "How's it going?" They answer, briefly, but honestly: "I'm great! We just found out we're expecting!" or, "Not so great, my dad's sick and might need to go to a nursing home." Maybe even "Pretty good, just enjoying summer on the deck with a yummy drink." In turn, they may ask the same of you, and you can reply with your own brief update. Close with a sincere "great to see you, take care!"

What just happened was a legitimate, genuine experiencing of another person's life in real time. It's not secondary (through another person or channel), and not removed in time. In the moment, you have to find a way to connect with people. And in doing so, you help your business by being a good and present friend or relative.

Ask yourself: What predicates the need for real estate services? Answer: birth, death, illness, marriage, divorce, graduation, job relocation, promotion, job loss. All of these things are shared on social media. When that happens, we have the opportunity to engage with the people experiencing them in a completely genuine fashion. When I walk into the coffee shop each day, I don't do so with a sandwich board and a megaphone, advertising my business. I'm not abrasive. I'm simply there, caring what happens to the people around me. And that matters.

2. Instant Message

A second opportunity on Facebook occurs in the chance to interact with people more one-on-one, through instant messaging. Use the IM feature to engage in private conversation with a single individual. Everyone is busy, and the very idea of our busy-ness can make it feel like we don't have time for a phone conversation. But an IM conversation can take place before we've thought about being too busy. It can even happen while we're doing other things.

When I IM with someone in my sphere, my goal is for the recipient to have two experiences: 1) they will leave the conversation feeling great, and 2) they will appreciate the connection, even though if they are too busy to accept the coffee date I suggest at the end. And ideally, a third thing will occur: 3) though I made no overt reference to buying or selling real estate for them, I have subliminally reinforced in the person's mind the fact that I sell real estate. This, plus the fact that they like me, subconsciously connects me with a potential future need.

3. Take it Off(line)

Sometimes the best way to manage your social media is to move beyond social media. If there's a birth, death, marriage, graduation, or whatever, you may learn about this via Facebook, but reach out by sending a card. Have good quality greeting cards on hand to send out. Consider always having a stack of cards that read "Just a Note" and are blank inside. Blank cards can be tailored to the situation, so always have them available for immediate use. I handwrite a brief note, and sign it. "Congratulations on the new job, well deserved!"; "My deepest condolences on the loss of your dad. Please let me know if there is anything I can do to help. You're in my thoughts."

These noteworthy events often also coincide with people buying or selling a home. But that's not what this is about. No real estate agent should become an ambulance chaser. You need to be human, and connect with people in a true way. Real estate is a service people need when they need it. You can simply say, "If there's anything I can do, please let me know." Implicit in your message is, *I don't sell something you don't need; I provide a service that you need. Let me help you.*

After I've said congratulations or condolences, I wait for two to four weeks before checking back. Then, I'll call to check in on how things are going and let them know how I can help, in a genuine way, from a place of concern and care. When you approach these situations in this way, you've left the person with a lasting impression of who you are.

Beyond Organic:
Some guidelines to posting online as your business.

So, how does this break down in terms of managing your contacts? You can refer back to the previous chapter to review how you reach your goal number of transactions, and how many contacts that will require. Facebook communication counts as one of these contacts. Every 60 days, you should touch your entire list of friends/contacts. Once you are consistently engaging your friends/contacts on their posts, develop a plan to engage using your own posts.

Only a small percentage of your fans interact with your posts when they show up in their newsfeed. The fans who don't click on your posts stop seeing you there, as social media algorithms filter out what is calculated to be "uninteresting."

That means your Facebook page isn't going to be seen by all your fans. In fact, Facebook said in February of 2012 that the average page was reaching just 12 percent of its fans. So, if you want your fans to see your posts, you need to get them to click on something in each post. That's why you hear so much about tactics to get people to like, share and comment on posts.

Shareability is all about what the post does to people. It affects them in such a way that they want to share with others. Highly shareable posts do at least one of the following:

- **GIVE:** Offers, discounts, deals or contests that everyone can benefit from, not just one sub-group of your friends. Local businesses benefit from this shareability, and it may create opportunity for you to build additional connections.
- **ADVISE:** Tips, especially about problems or topics that apply to a large audience. Examples include how prep your home for fall, community recycling programs, school sports schedules.
- **INFORM:** News stories about the communities you live in, or stories that have broad concern, or warnings about dangers that could affect anyone.
- **ENTERTAIN:** Funny pictures and quotes. Create a photo contest with your listings, signs or marketing material. Have you ever played: "Caption this picture"?
- **INSPIRE:** Inspirational quotes or images. When used sparingly, this gives people insight to your personality and creates connection points.
- **AMAZE:** Amazing pictures or facts.

- **ACKNOWLEDGEMENT:** Giving credit where credit is due. Vendors, affiliates, clients all need and want accolades.
- **REAL ESTATE:** Posting business-specific content can be tricky. However, it is important to relay this information from time to time. If you find a good article, give a synopsis of the topic and then link the article. Use video to provide pertinent, sharable info directly from you. Post searches directly from your website, encouraging people to become familiar with your brand and site.

To get an idea how important proper Facebook protocol can be, consider this story: imagine you had purchased a car, and the salesperson, whom you really liked, connected with you on a social media platform. After your purchase, that salesperson posts daily about new cars, better features than the ones you just bought, and their newest big sales. How would this impact your experience? Might you end up feeling less positive about your recent purchase? Might you end up resenting the person you once liked, who is now reminding you of how inferior your new car is?

This is actually a real-world example that happened to me. After several posts that left me feeling bad about my new car and the person who sold it to me, I reached out to offer my feedback. Kayla changed her approach, and started sending me things that mattered to me—recall notices, free car wash, coupons, oil change discounts. She created the desire for another new car by getting me into the dealership, where I'd see other cars. And sure enough, I bought another car from her two years later.

Sharing on social media without a targeted plan can put

your relationships at risk. People may hide your updates, or disconnect from you entirely. The experience with Kayla the Car Salesperson gave me a clear picture of how people want to be interacted with on Facebook. It also taught me how, by following an engagement strategy, Kayla made me a client for life. She continued to follow up with me in a way that was about me, not about her.

Apply that same line of thinking to your real estate clients. Providing content to enrich the home they have, while at the same time remaining top of mind, creates an opportunity to serve them when the time is right for a new home

Follow-Up Cycle

Follow-up is singularly *the* largest point of atrophy in the typical agent's business. We talk about using a CRM as a tool to manage your contacts (*see, e.g.*, p. 191). The greatest thing about a contact management system is its ability to track your metrics, allowing you to judge success and failure objectively, leading to better results. But before you can use this tool, let's step back and identify how the follow-up cycle works.

A few years ago, my sales team was struggling. I was holed up in a conference room with a whiteboard, trying to track our work and visually identify where each member of the team was stumbling or outright failing. What I found changed my life and my profitability.

We started by tracking the clients we had had success in converting to closed sales, and compared similarities among these clients. We used a linear visual model to identify and map the steps in the process from lead to closed transaction. Overwhelmingly, we found that there are **six steps to each successful conversion**. Through this mapping exercise, it became evident where each of my agents was struggling.

1. The First Touch:
The first contact can come in any number of ways: meeting at an event, meeting at an open house, a sign call, an internet lead, a personal referral, etc. Some initial contact sources have better overall conversion rates than others, but the process and approach to following up should be the same. After the first formative contact, add the person to your database. Make sure to take good notes regarding the specifics of the conversation or exchange. This will become important later as you build rapport.

2. First Follow-Up:
Depending upon the manner of the first contact, the way you first follow up may vary. But follow-up is critical, nonetheless. Make every effort to reach out to your new contact sooner rather than later, to solidify the connection and build on the first contact. For my team, handwritten notes have worked really well at this step.

3. Second Follow-Up:
At this step in the process, my team's goal was to set an appointment to meet face-to-face. This step may require multiple contacts—phone calls, emails, notes and instant messages. Unless they tell you they aren't interested, continue to reach out until you can schedule a meeting.

The objective is to continue building rapport. Maintaining contact and keeping communication is paramount to successful conversion. This can be accomplished in a number of ways, and the meeting you arrange should reflect your understanding of their needs. For example, you can offer to meet at their house to determine its potential value if they choose to list with you. Have the buyer meet you at your office to discuss the home-buying process, and educate them. Invite them to an open house or a community event. Or, simply ask them to coffee.

4. Meeting:

When you do meet in person, be sure to refer back to your initial notes as a refresher. At the meeting, reiterate high points of your last contact with them. This gives the potential client a chance to confirm and clarify their needs and wants. This is also the step in the process where you can map out a timeline and expectations for them.

Many times, at this point, the potential client is ready to move forward, whether it's starting to look at homes to buy, or listing their home. Realize this opportunity and close the deal. Read body language and verbal cues, and determine their level of comfort.

5. Third Follow-up:

Use the two-meeting approach to building long-term clients. In this approach, **the third follow-up is the most important**—and is usually the failure point.

Depending on the client, you may already be showing them homes or preparing to list their current home at this point. But, if they're still not committed, you have to continue making positive contact. Usually, we achieved this through emails and phone calls. The contact was friendly yet informative. Remember to keep taking notes.

6. Conversion meeting:

This is the step that determines the success of the other parts of the process. By now, you've made every effort to show your desire to work with the potential client, your area expertise and your overall knowledge. You have also shown them your commitment.

You can track your conversion ratio at this point. If you map out your own history with your follow-up efforts, you can identify your success and failure points. The points of failure may emerge from a number of things. Some questions to ask yourself as you assess your process include:

- Are you in contact with enough people?
- Do you need practice on your scripts? Try role-playing face-to-face and over the phone.
- Did you follow up as needed, and was the follow-up geared toward the specific potential client?
- What questions did you ask, and what should you have asked?
- Did you close the sale when appropriate?

THE REAL ESTATE

EVENT

FIRST CONTACT

- COMMUNITY EVENT
- CHARITY EVENT
- OPEN HOUSE
- FIRST TIME H.B SEMINAR

FIRST TOUCH

FIRST FOLLOW-UP

- HANDWRITTEN NOTE
- ADD TO DATABASE W/ NOTES
- EMAIL
- PHONE CALL

CLOSING

SHOWING HOMES & LISTING PROPERTIES.

MAKE SURE YOU DO WHAT YOU COMMITED TO DO.

COMMUNICATED ANY DEVIATION AND ASK FOR REFERRALS.

FOLLOW-UP CYCLE

EXTENDED

SECOND TOUCH

GOAL TO SET APPOINTMENT.
THIS MAY TAKE MULTIPLE
ATTEMPTS OVER WEEKS.

- PHONE CALLS
- INSTANT MESSAGES
- PERSONAL EMAILS
- BUILD RAPPORT

MEETING OR SUBSTANTIVE CONVERSATION

MAKE SURE YOU ARE PREPARED.

USE NOTES FROM PREVIOUS
CONVOS/MEETING TO CAPITALIZE
ON RAPPORT. IDENTIFY AND
REITERATE THEIR NEEDS.

Chapter 7: Going Beyond Your Sphere—Network Referrals

Marketing Beyond Your Sphere

As we've stated, your sphere of influence (including past client referrals) will typically account for between 65 and 80 percent of your business. This percentage will rise the longer you've been in business, as you will naturally get more volume from previous client referrals and repeat clients. It's of primary importance, and cost-effective, to nurture this resource to keep it strong and growing.

But what about the other 20 to 35 percent of your business? Not to mention the opportunities to increase your business at a faster rate than the longer-term growth that comes from your sphere? There are numerous additional marketing methods and prospecting tools you can use to increase your sales volume. Most common examples include:

- Social Media
- Business Networking

- REALTOR®-to- REALTOR®-Referrals
- Convention Strategy
- Internet Leads
- Website
- Geo Farming
- Expired Listings
- Direct Mail
- For Sale By Owner
- Open Houses
- Door-Knocking
- Relocation
- Home Buyer Seminars
- Blog Writing
- Print Advertisements

Keep in mind that you should under no circumstances attempt to cover all of these strategies at once. It will be much more profitable to read through this section with an intent to assess which approach you think will work best for you based on your time, available financial resources, personality, and general preferences. Once you have zeroed in on the method you'd like to use first, it's best to get a really good handle on what you'll need to do to make that method work by setting up a plan, and executing that plan for at least one full year.

After one year, take time to review precisely what worked, what it cost you in time and money, and your percentage of closed transactions relative to your efforts. From there, you'll have valuable data to help you refine your approach each year going forward, and you'll be able to become much more effective and focused. Real numbers always help! Guesswork and wishes, not so much.

In the meantime, don't get discouraged, and don't blame

the method if it isn't working for you. Often, the reason behind a lack of anticipated success can be attributed to either inadequate investment or incomplete follow-through. Hold yourself accountable for the consistent efforts you will need to put forth. And recognize that you are building your skills, knowledge, and business results for a longer game. Sticking with your work will pay off over time; abandoning your plan ensures you'll get nothing.

The Art of Networking

Mary Kay Ash, founder of Mary Kay Cosmetics, once said, "Everyone has an invisible sign hanging from their neck saying, *'Make me feel important.'*" Will the next person you meet change your life? They could! Or you could well change theirs.

Real estate is a relationship business, built on who you know and who knows you. The sphere of people you already know comprises your most valuable resource, and you want to be growing that resource all the time. The essence of *expanding* your universe of people you know can be summed up in a word: networking.

A skilled networker is always striking up conversation (perhaps at times to the dismay of their waiting family and friends). Networking for real estate agents requires one essential skill: the ability to listen. If you can master this, networking gold can be yours.

There are different types of opportunities to meet people, and different ways to approach them. Learning to recognize and make the most of the opportunities in front of you is potentially the best way to make new connections and expand your business.

Chance Encounters

There's a good chance you meet one to three people each day. The stylist at the salon, the receptionist at the clinic where you took your sick child, or the server taking your lunch order. Have you ever taken the opportunity to talk to them? Most people willingly offer up telling life details to complete strangers, in passing conversation. Usually, once engaged, they'll ask about you, too.

If you were to take a few extra minutes every day to engage these chance encounters, you would "meet" more than 500 additional people every year—people who can, and will, change your life.

Creating a lasting impression comes down to listening, and determining: *Can I be of help to this person in some way?* Maybe it's just a moment of connection, or maybe they need a good mechanic, or a good computer tech, a tutor, or just a restaurant suggestion. If you're able to help them, you have completed the networking trifecta: you win, they win, and you made a new connection! Keep a notebook or use the note section on your phone to record all your chance encounters. Whether you choose to follow up with each of them is not the objective of this exercise. The goal is to make you aware of all the opportunity you have around you.

Planned Encounters

Networking events and conventions are commonplace in real estate. There is no shortage of opportunity to meet and engage fellow industry people. Meeting the right people and having the right conversations is the goal. Creating rapport is the challenge.

As our lives become more digital, in-person networking can feel increasingly awkward. Walking into an event where you know no one and introducing yourself to a stranger is intimidating, even if you are an extrovert. But the truth remains, it's all about *who you know*. So, maximizing your time and connections is critically important.

Who should you know? When you find yourself at an event, look for two people:

- 1) the person who knows everyone, and
- 2) the person standing alone in the corner.

Each of these people has something to offer you, and you them. The person who knows everyone will make introductions, and usually will impart tidbits along the way, allowing you to understand and navigate the waters more easily. And that person standing in the corner? They are equally important. This relationship often becomes the strongest, because you serve their needs as well as yours.

I once met a man at an event. We were both attending the event alone, and walked in at the same time. He was nervous, I could tell, but he meant business. I introduced myself to him as we walked toward the door, and asked if he knew any one at the event. He responded, "I do now." We both laughed and proceeded into the lounge.

Over the course of the evening, I watched my new friend as he worked the room. He was thoughtful and engaged. He listened, and only spoke when asked a question. His elevator speech was polished, but not overdone. He asked people, "I appreciate your insight, would you mind if I was to follow up with you later?"

At the end of the evening, I made an effort speak to him again. I told him I was impressed, maybe even a little jealous of how well he worked the room. He replied, "It was easy, I knew you!"

He was *good!* He made me feel just as connected as every person he had met that night, and did it with a compliment. He went on to say, "I'm an introvert by nature, so I have to stick to an action plan, or I would end up hiding out in the parking garage, listening to sports talk radio all night."

Each time you meet someone new, don't forget to follow up! This is where too many agents fail. You had a connection, got their contact information, and then took no action. That is a missed opportunity, and you'll never know how much of an impact that person might have had on your business - or on your life.

Have an action plan in place before attending an event, so that you are ready to make the most of the opportunity placed before you.

Key Points to remember when entering a room at a networking event or conference:

- Set a goal to meet at least **five new people.**
- **Listen**—by listening, you have a better chance to identify points of connection and ways you may be able to help someone.
- Have a compelling **"elevator" speech**—no more than 90 seconds long. Adapt your message to your audience. Your elevator speech should include a problem, a solution, and how it affects the person you're talking to.
- Don't just exchange cards! Sure, you mean well,

and you want to connect with that person in the future. So make the future happen now: take their email address or phone number, and **send them a message on the spot**. Make a comment about something the two of you discussed, and acknowledge how nice it was to meet them.

Industry Connections

The average real estate transaction creates $56,000 in additional expenditures to the economy. Parties involved in a typical home sale might include a mortgage company, a title company, an inspector, an appraiser, a lawyer, a contractor, a handyman, a mover, an appliance delivery guy...the list goes on. Each of the people connected to your client's move could provide a great next referral, or even become a career-long referral source for your business.

Approach these contacts in much the same way you would other networking connections, by building them into your professional sphere and being attuned to how you can be of service to them. Professionals also appreciate the referral value of someone they know, like and trust. Don't just assume you're that person—*ask* them to send you business, and let them know you'll be referring people to them as well.

Industry partners are an extension of your business. Thus, their service is a reflection of your service. Aligning yourself with the right network of people is crucial to your success. Seek out people and companies with a similar mindset, work ethic, and approach to the customer. The right connections within the industry will add value to everyone's business.

Convention Strategy

One valuable type of industry connection is with real estate professionals in other locations. I developed a strategy to connect with agents in other states that worked very effectively for me at the RE/MAX International Convention.

The annual RE/MAX convention is held in late February or early March. In early- to mid-January, I would visit my state real estate archives. Every state has one of these, and most of the time, the needed data is online - and all of the information is free. Contained in the state archives is demographic information about who moves in and out of your state. I would figure out the top five states with the most people moving to mine.

With this information in hand, I'd go through the national register of people from RE/MAX, and search Facebook, LinkedIn and Twitter for agents from these states. I'd reach out to these agents to see if they were heading to the convention (or if they knew anyone who might be going from their area). If not, I had at least made a personal connection with an agent in another city/state who most likely would come into contact with someone moving to my area. I immediately followed up with a hand-written note thanking them for their help and taking time to converse with me. I also put their name and contact information in my Agent-to-Agent Database (or ATAD).

If I did happen upon an agent coming to the convention, I would make plans to meet them for coffee or at an outing during the conference. Again, a hand-written note thanking them for taking the time to talk and reaffirming our plans to meet was sent right away, and their name and contact information was added to the ATAD.

When the convention day arrived, I had committed the five states that I should concentrate on to memory. Every time I saw one of these states on a nametag at a social event, awards night, educational session, or in line waiting to buy coffee, I would strike up a conversation. I was direct. "Oh hi, you are from Oregon! There are quite a few people that move from Oregon to Minnesota every year. Let's exchange information so that I can send you referrals and you can do the same." I'd collect their business card at that time. If they forgot business cards (a sin at a convention) or had run out, I would jot down their name and contact information on a small pad of paper I carried with me.

That night, while everyone else was out on the town, I'd sit down with all of the cards and pages of notepaper I had collected throughout the day. I'd write each person a handwritten note, thanking them for their time at the convention, and telling them how much I looked forward to working with them in the future. I also mentioned in that note that I might like to come visit their office sometime and meet the agents with whom they worked. Of course, I would then add each of these agents to my ATAD.

I did this intensely every day of the convention. I'd pack several hundred note cards for this purpose. However, I didn't mail the cards from the convention, because I wanted them to have my local postmark. And I wanted the agents to receive their cards about three or four days after they had returned home.

Then came part two. After about a month had passed, I started calling the agents I had met at the convention. I started to categorize these agents as As, Bs, and Cs:

- A C agent was a nice agent with whom I had a positive

connection, but who did not have a lot of influence or relationships within their office, and did not come in contact with many people moving to my area. They went in to my ATAD for a substantive contact every six months.

- A B rating resulted from a good interaction, with a potential for having referrals moving to my area, but was an agent who was not a great influencer or relationship hub for his or her fellow agents. This agent would get a substantive contact from me once a quarter.
- The A agents were really important because they sent me the most business. They were those few agents who had influence in their offices and were relationship hubs for other agents. They also were aware that people from their area moved to my area, and they were committed to building a referral relationship with me. The A agents got a substantive contact from me once a month.

Additionally, I called the A agents and let them know I'd like to come visit them. I let them know that I wanted to tour their office and even meet their manager/owner when I was in town. I'd book a flight and spend a day in whatever state the A agent resided. It was always lots of fun. I'd usually have breakfast with the A agent, and then go tour their office. Often, I'd arrive on the day they held their weekly office meeting. I'd meet all of the other agents and the manager/owner, if possible.

As I met each person in the office, I gave them my card, and also collected theirs. I'd usually suggest taking them all out to lunch or dinner that day. That night, back at the hotel, I'd write a hand-written note to every single agent I had met that day, and I'd put them in my ATAD. I'd mail the notes when I got back home. Weeks later, I would classify each of these new agents I had met as an A, B, or C and the entire cycle would start over again. (For more about categorizing your database, see Chapter 6.)

This went on for years. My ATAD grew and grew. It got so big and so connected that I would recognize, and be recognized by, many people at every yearly convention. I even started holding my own parties at a nearby hotel for my entire ATAD.

Every three months, I combed through my ATAD and deleted names of people who were not giving me any referrals over time, and did not have influence with other agents. I also moved agents from A to B, C to B, etc. depending on the referrals I'd gained from the. I found that 500 members in this database was a healthy amount to maintain. Moreover, I found that I could count on a ratio of 10 percent closed transactions on a yearly basis relative to the number of ATAD members. When my ATAD had grown to a solid 500 agents from around the country (and the world), I could count on 50 closed transactions per year!

Right about now, skeptical readers are wondering, "How did you happen to find so many people who knew other people moving to your area?" Seems incredible doesn't it?

Recall in Chapter 6, when we talked about the Reticular Activating System. Remember the phenomenon of never noticing a Volvo S60 on the road until you test-drove one, and then suddenly seeing them everywhere? My ATAD worked a lot like this. Often, agents never noticed how many people moved to my area until I started pointing it out to them.

I can't tell you how many times I heard, "What in the world is happening? Why is everyone suddenly moving to Minneapolis?"

Of course, the reality was that the number of people moving to my area was no higher than usual. What had changed was the agent now had a reason to take note of it. That's the Reticular Activating System in action, and that's how it helped me build a valuable professional referral network.

Compounding Effect

Networking results will naturally ebb and flow. Expanding the number of people you know leads to increased referral opportunities. But it can be difficult to track the specific return of any given connection, because the overall picture of networking is more of a web than a straight, reciprocal line from one person to another.

Keep in mind that there is a compounding effect when you add new people to your sphere. As a general rule you can assume that each person you meet knows three people who will buy or sell a home in the coming year.

For example, if you attend 13 events in a year, with the goal of meeting five new people at each, you would meet 65 new professional people over the course of the year. It seems manageable to add 65 people to your database, and follow up with them. You'll need to set up 65 coffee dates, because someone is not a referral partner until and unless they know enough about you, and you about them, to trust your professionalism. But once you've connected, you can potentially expect to gain three leads a year from each new resource. If you happen to have the gift of gab, and connect to more people in a shorter period of time, you may have a higher conversion rate.

But in order for this to bear fruit, you need to be very purposeful and consistent in your approach. You'll need to follow through on your commitment to attend all the events you said you would, you need to show up with intention and meet five people each time, and you need to follow up.

Once I've met someone, I do one of two things. I try to connect on some digital platform. I'll see if they're on Facebook, and ask to connect there. I actually take out my phone, and hand it to them so they can give me their contact info on the spot. That way, when I leave the event I'm already on top of my game, rather than going home and having to figure out what to do with a card.

You may want to make use of technology for taking contact information. Programs like Evernote can be very useful. Evernote has a card-reading feature which scans the information into your phone, allows you to record where you met the person, and adds them to your contacts.

After a networking event, it is crucial to follow up with each new person you met. Connecting on a social media platform like Facebook can give you a three-dimensional understanding of who people are, offering information well beyond just a name. You can also send a text message, an email, instant message, or hand-written note.

Then add each new connection to your database, including them in your follow-up touches, just like anyone else in your sphere. If you take a systematic approach to making new contacts and following up, you develop the ability to duplicate your results year after year.

Chapter 8: Internet Leads and Your Website

Internet Leads

Internet leads are a vast and frequently misunderstood source of real estate leads. You want to drive curious potential buyers and sellers from various places around the internet, to *your* website (note, not your broker's). There, they may sign up to have you contact them, and you can set up a time to meet and answer their questions and let them know how you can help them. Remember the process we discussed in chapter 5

Leads → Contacts → Appointments → Sales

The internet is a giant sea of possibility. But because of its vastness, a lot of leads need to make it through the pipeline to result in a single sale. Typically, you can assume a success rate of 1 percent - that is to say, for every 100 internet leads, you will get one transaction.

So, how do you get these leads?

Sources of internet leads break down into some basic categories: purchased ads on real estate websites, lead generation websites, pay-per-click ads, and broker-referred leads. Each has its own strategy, costs, and pros and cons.

Purchased Ads

One way to drive leads to your website is to purchase ads on third-party real estate websites, such as Zillow, Trulia, Homes.com, or Realtor.com. Most of these sites require you purchase the opportunity to be one of up to three agents posted on the page being viewed by potential homebuyers, who are beginning their search via these sites. Searches, and ads, are based on zip codes. The person viewing the page may or may not click on your ad, and from there, may or may not sign up on your website.

One thing to keep in mind when planning a strategy around these ads is that people who peruse these sites will be at a wide range of readiness to become actual buyers. Some people like to look at for-sale houses just for fun. Some might be looking for valuation information for their own house. Some might be looking seriously, but still be six months to a year from buying. Some might be interested, but lack the financial ability to buy. And, of course, some will be ready to pull the trigger right away. You'll encounter all of these people. Some will be interested in talking to you, and some won't.

Most typical is the potential buyer who is about six months from an actual purchase. This can present an opportunity, in that if you connect with people at this point, you can be the one they have in mind as they get more serious in their process. This type of lead will require much more follow up and education to woo the buyers, and it can be time-intensive to convert leads like this. It can take eight to ten follow-up contacts before someone decides to work with you. I've also had the experience of making eight to ten contacts with someone, and had them *not* sign with me, either because they go with someone else, or because they don't buy at all.

In addition, immediacy of response is critical to making an impression with these leads. Generally, a potential win goes to the agent who reaches the customer first.

Usually, sites like Zillow will require an annual contract that you cannot get out of early. You can purchase a predetermined number of views per zip code, or you can purchase an entire zip code in order to be the only agent to appear in the searches of that area. Zip code prices will vary by region based on supply and demand. This cost may be easier for larger teams and agents whom are already productive to absorb. They may have the resources to buy entire territories so as to capture all leads. Being the only ad tends to be more successful, because you can generate a larger quantity of leads, and you have no competition.

Remember, with a 1% conversion rate you need 100 leads to get 1 sale. So, unless you get 100 or more leads, any internet lead approach may not necessarily be worth pursuing. Generally, until you are able to go 'all in' and commit the amount of time and money necessary to yield results, there is too much competition out there for it to be worthwhile.

Lead Generation Websites

The next methodology of online lead generation is to utilize pre-built websites with your branding powered by pay-per-click ads. Examples of these include Real Estate Webmasters,

Househunt.com, Commissions Inc., Boomtown, Kunversion and Tiger Leads. They typically have strong calls to action and high conversion rates to get visitors to register.

These sites are basically 'shovel-ready.' They are set up for you, branded with your information, and licensed to you. The service is contract-based, and more expensive than purchased ads. But in some cases, they can guarantee the number of leads you will get. You'll need to have a larger budget to commit to this approach. Costs may start at about $500 per month, but most effective lead generation website budgets are closer to $2,000 per month.

Lead generation sites used to be the best way to get leads, because these companies are so good at driving the traffic to agents. However, as more companies have jumped into the fray, there are now many websites that are so similar it's hard to get exclusive leads. Sites can't guarantee that consumers haven't registered at other websites, so even when you do get a lead, it might be a prospective client who has already been contacted by someone else.

Broker-Referred Leads

You may also get leads from your broker, which come through the brokerage website. Usually, these leads come with a referral fee. However, while a fee of 25 percent may sound high, this is actually a great deal because you pay only for leads that end in a sale.

Your Website

It is extremely important that your website be a reflection of who you are and the services you offer. Consider your website your central business hub, to which all of your marketing should flow. This is where consumers will go to learn more about you and your company, search for homes, and read testimonials.

You want to stand out from your competition, and that means not having the exact same website as every other agent at your brokerage. If you do use the website provided by your brokerage, at least customize the pages to reflect your individual style.

Purchasing a domain name is a simple, cost-effective way for consumers to be able to find you more quickly. If you think that the average person will type in yourbrokersname.com/yourname, you're wrong. Consumers likely are not conscious of the broker relationship, or of the significance of connecting to your specific website, and they will just go to your broker's site. Having a web domain consistent with your name, brand or local area will help consumers find you.

Since it is *your* website, you should build and host it yourself, or hire someone to do this for you. Make sure you own the content, and are the sole beneficiary of all of your hard work. You don't want to build on rented land, and you don't want to build up someone else's SEO, only to have them take it when you either switch brokerages or stop paying for that service.

There are many real estate website companies that offer a full range of services. Picking the right one depends on your budget, technological savvy, and goals. Think about what you need, and how much time you're willing to invest before you make a decision.

I personally spend about 10 hours a week maintaining our team's website and creating new original content, including blog posts. This keeps the viewers engaged and coming back to revisit the website. It also keeps the website fresh in the eyes of search engines, as I'm always adjusting content to match popular search terms.

At a bare minimum, your website should have information about you, and a way for the consumer to contact you. You may also want to have a testimonial page that highlights real reviews from your past clients. Most real estate websites include a way to look at local listings, either through an IDX provider, or via a link to their broker's home search function.

Real estate is local, and your website is a great place for you to demonstrate your knowledge of the local market. If you're adept at writing, blogs are a great way to engage your audience and talk about what is going on in your community.

Maximizing your website: Pay-Per-Click vs. SEO

When it comes to generating traffic, there are two philosophies, you can buy pay-per-click ads that will send people to your landing page. This gives you the ability to quickly ramp up and start getting traffic from day one however requires continual investment in an ad budget. The second option involves attracting customers organically, by having content that comes up when people search online. This is called search engine optimization (SEO).

If you're serious about generating leads in the long run, you'll need to really focus on organic traffic. However, some people don't have the time or don't know how to create original content, and would prefer to just pay for traffic. There's nothing wrong with this. You just need to know how to get the best bang for your buck.

Achieving the top spot on Google may not be realistic, companies like Zillow have invested millions of dollars and have an army of people creating content for them. Not to mention the size of their advertising budget. The key to success is to focus on hyper-local content. Go after the long-tail keywords about things that are local. Create content on your website that is tailored to what your audience is looking for, so when they search, your site comes up.

You can pay people to create this type of content. This can backfire if the person you hire isn't local (*very* local, even, if you're talking about a neighborhood) and knowledgeable. Additionally, most places that sell content are selling you language that isn't unique to you. And consumers don't really care about the generalized information delivered by this type of mass content creation. What they want to know is local information, and how it affects them. When you write and post your own content, you are in control and can incorporate the details you want clients to see.

Also, when you invest in your own content, you will have it for years to come, so it's always working for you even when you're not paying for it. With pay-per-click, you need to constantly spend money. And once your ad budget is used up, that's all you get. Ultimately the best approach is a hybrid of the two, to drive traffic and convert leads at a successful rate.

Content marketing is all about creating original content that the reader values. A lot of people go wrong by copying and pasting others' works, or just regurgitating what someone else has already said. It is important that what you talk about is relevant to your reader, and to your overall goal of selling real estate. You could write all day about your favorite movies, recipes, etc., but that will not help you sell homes.

Buyers want to read about different neighborhoods, and what amenities areas have to offer. Schools are very important, so providing buyers with quick links to boundary maps and information about the different schools in the area is very helpful. You can pair this with active listings by using an IDX provider. This way, when buyers are interested in a particular elementary school, they will be able to find homes in that area.

Sellers want to know what techniques are important to selling their home. If homes in a particular area are selling quickly and for more money, those homeowners would be interested to read about it. Are you doing something different than your competitors to market properties? Write about it!

Consumers are out there surfing the web right now, and if you have original content to offer, they will want to read it. Content marketing for real estate is a great way to capture buyers' and sellers' attention before they enter the marketplace.

You can also drive traffic to your website by purchasing pay-per-click (PPC) ads. Google and Facebook are the two most popular sites for this type of marketing. You can do this yourself, or hire out to a company like Curyator whom are experts at creating the copy and managing the ad budget.

The most common pay-per-click (PPC) type of advertising is Google AdWords. It is very easy to set up, and the folks over at Google will help you for free anytime. Don't fall for companies that claim to be "Google's number one partner," or promise you a certain amount of traffic or placement. Google AdWords will help you identify potential search keywords, and give you an idea of average cost per click and potential traffic.

Typical cost per click for popular real estate terms here in the Twin Cities can be up to $5 a click. We do not recommend spending money on general, popular real estate keywords. This can become quite costly due to the amount of competition.

Generally, the more specific the ad is, the more effective it's going to be. For example, instead of bidding on "Homes for sale in Maple Grove," bid on "Homes for sale in Nottingham neighborhood Maple Grove." There will be less competition for this search, and thus a much lower cost-per-click. Also, the consumer searching that specific phrase has likely already narrowed down their criteria, and is a more serious buyer.

A calculated method for utilizing pay-per-click ads is to purchase long-tail keywords, and then direct the consumer to a landing page related to that topic. For instance, if someone is looking for a particular school, send them to a page about that school. Currently within our MLS here in Minnesota, there is not a good way to search by elementary schools, neighborhoods, or a specific lake a buyer might want to be on. There either isn't a required field for it, or the agents whom have inputted their listings did not fill it out properly. Consumers aren't able to find this type of information on the national websites either because they're relying on that same data feed. This gives us an opportunity to provide value to someone whom is looking for a home in a specific area. To the extent that we can capture this type of search through keywords, we can offer more customized information for the buyer, and designate ourselves as specialists in the area where they are looking. The landing pages of course will need to have the information the consumer is looking for, as well as property listings. This is done with a polygon tool through an IDX provider.

The internet database exchange, or IDX, allows you to display listings on your own website. It also gives you the capability to create content, like specific pages focusing on a particular school or neighborhood, with included listings matching that topic. Most buyers use the internet to search for homes, not for agents. Offering an easy way for them to find properties will result in leads, either through a squeeze page (a page that pops up and blocks you from going further until you put in information), or from inquires on individual listings.

There are a limited number of vendors who sell the ability to integrate data. Individual designers can set up your website with this feature. It's best to work with a designer who is familiar with building real estate websites in order to ensure proper functionality. Spending more on your website pays off, both in terms of the leads you're able to generate, as well as the control you have.

Create pages with embedded saved searches that are important to buyers, where their preferred search factors are captured. Examples include searches by schools, neighborhoods, new construction developments, specific condo buildings or lake homes. Having saved searches that complement your niche will promote you as an expert. Saved jump searches combined with original content are a great way to provide your viewers value. Once the pages have been created, they will automatically update as new listings come on the market. If you aren't sure how to set this up, you can hire someone to do it for you, and to train you how to make the best use of it. This can be costly, so make sure this strategy makes sense for your business.

In a world where connecting to the internet has become as common as your daily drive to the office or to show property, we know that the consumer is increasingly looking to the web for information on real estate. When building a real estate website, understanding what the consumer is searching for is vital.

Consumers aren't just looking for a property, they're looking for a place to live. Our goal in building a website should not be to give the consumer a place to *search* for homes, but to help them *find* a home. With this goal in mind, there are some important factors to consider.

The phrase "long tail keyword searches" sounds like a foreign language to most, but when having a website that converts leads is your goal, this is something you should consider daily. Consumers are no longer typing "Houston Homes For Sale" in search engines. Instead, they're typing "4 bedroom home for sale in (city name) with a pool." This is vital information to consider, but how do we make sure our sites are built to show up when these terms are used? Your IDX plays a big part, yes. But more importantly, you must create content about the parts of town you work, and leverage your IDX.

I would have you consider the terms that consumers are searching for, and build your pages accordingly. Depending on your IDX vendor, you have different ways to create what I call "Evergreen Searches." These are pages that will refresh and update based on changes in the MLS, but are static as far as the search criteria. These pre-set searches will give the consumer exactly what they're looking for, and highlight those pages.

In research I have done, I've observed that pages that are more specific to particular search criteria (pool, golf course, etc.) receive up to 40 percent more search traffic than generic searches (e.g., homes in a particular price range in a certain part of town), which is what most agents and brokers build first into their website.

The best way to spend your time and effort on a website is to give consumers the ability to *find* what they are looking for, instead of just searching with the hope of finding something. Use your local area expertise to create a site focusing on specific search criteria for the people trusting your site to guide them where they want to go.

Ryan Bokros is a REALTOR® and Managing Director at Bamboo Realty in Houston, Texas with 12 years of industry experience. He has been a real estate technology consultant for many years, and helps agents and brokers leverage technology in their business.

Lead Capture Rates

Pay attention to how much you're paying, and what percentage of people visiting your website become leads by completing the form and sending you their contact information (your ***lead capture rate***). When paying per click, it becomes important to know how many people will sign up. A website that is well-designed, contains good content, and has a strong call to action should get you a 10% rate of sign-up. If you're seeing traffic flow to your landing page, but people are not signing up, you should look at your website.

Sometimes, too, there can be something else going on. For instance, at one point, I noticed that I was getting only 1 in 700 leads captured from the traffic to my site. When I investigated, I found that a large volume of that traffic was coming from Alabama, and I'm in Minnesota. I realized that there was a community with the same name as the neighborhood I was using for my keywords, and so people were clicking through and landing on my site, but then not signing up because I wasn't what they needed. This told me I needed to further modify my search terms.

I've also noticed that increased traffic often correlates with times I've written blog posts, which turned out to be agents, not leads. The upshot is, pay attention to your lead capture rates to help maximize your investment in ads. You don't need to be paying for people to click through who are not potential clients.

Response

Regardless of the source of your internet leads, your response timing needs to be nearly immediate—under a minute is best. Follow-up is crucial, as well. This is where contact management comes in.

I recommend a system called Follow-Up Boss. You can set this to dial your phone right away when you get a lead, and when you answer, it will inform you of the new lead and the phone number to call. You can also set it up to text the customer immediately, and ask when the best time to call them is. Consumers may not necessarily need an answer right away, but what they do need is an acknowledgement that their question will be answered soon. By reaching out immediately, you are meeting this need.

Our team has a dedicated buyer's agent, whose entire job is to follow up with leads. We divide up the process, and I handle generating the leads. Whether you're doing the whole thing yourself, or divvying up the duties, I recommend that you use a contact management system to keep on top of the response and follow-up calls. After all, you spend money generating the lead, it's important to commit the time and focus needed to making the most of it. Otherwise, you're wasting money and opportunity.

When I reach out to new leads, what I find to be most effective is to bring them into the office and walk them through the home-buying process. At this time, you can find out if they are pre-approved and ready, willing and able to become buyers. If they won't come in, this generally indicates they aren't as serious, or may be earlier in their process.

Most internet leads are going to be first-time homebuyers, in part because younger generations are more inclined to start their process on the internet. If you can get someone to meet with you, you're statistically approximately 75% to a sale. It's easier to gain trust with people in person, to interact in real time, and your conversion rate is going to go up from there.

But a lot of people won't even answer the phone. Remember that what we're talking about here is leads, and our job is to follow them. If the answer is 'no' with a particular lead, be thankful that you're now one lead closer to your 100th—and a sale!

Things to keep in mind regarding your response to all internet leads:

- Follow up, and follow up fast
- Ask open-ended questions
- Follow up again
- Provide value
- Remember this is about them, not you

Lead Conversion

Overall, there are many different sources from which to get internet leads, and ways to convert leads, but need you'll need to look at each one individually, to determine what is working best for you. At end of year, review how many sales you made, in order to determine your cost per sale. Look at how many views, how many clicks, how many leads, and how many leads turned into a sale, as well as how much this all cost you, and assess where the issues were.

Consider your break-even point to assess whether it's a worthwhile investment of your time and money to pursue this method. When you're newer in the industry, or newer to a particular strategy, you may be in a position to have a lower rate of return while you get your name out and build your business. On the other hand, if you're a team leader, and you need to have enough leads for everyone to get what they need, with enough left over for you to get paid, that's a different set of considerations. Similarly, in some markets, fewer leads will generate more return because of higher home prices.

For most people who pursue this method, internet leads will account for 5-10% of their business. The vast majority of agents don't go after internet leads at all. A select few individuals have been very successful with this approach, with internet leads representing upwards of 50% of their business.

Whatever you do, make sure that you understand the industry standards for conversion, so that you aren't upset when 99 people don't call you back. Remember that statistically, there is a 'yes' for every 99 'no's, so remind yourself that for every 'no,' you're one closer to your 'yes'. Don't take it personally. Commit to the process and see it all the way through, or don't do it.

Chapter 9: Geo-Farming

What is geo-farming?

A geo-farm is a defined geographic area of households to which you send monthly mailings over the course of a year, with the specific goal of increasing your number of listings. You will need to determine an area that has a high likelihood of homeownership turnover, and then create awareness and familiarity among members of the community. Through that effort, you should become a real estate agent of choice within that area. This is a method that takes time and commitment, but can be very rewarding.

Identifying the farm

The first thing you'll need to do is identify an area to farm. It should be close enough to your home or office that you're able to keep an eye on what is going on there and provide the best level of service. Many agents will farm the neighborhood they live in; though it's worth bearing in mind that some sellers will not want a neighbor knowing their personal information.

It can be a mistake to select an area based solely on a high price point, or just because you've lived in that neighborhood. These choices can be driven either by the misconception that more money per transaction should be your main goal, or by an emotionally-based attachment to an area. Neither motivation necessarily translates into a good foundation for your geo-farm area. You'll want to make a more thorough assessment of some important factors to determine if a given area will likely net you good return on your investment of time and money.

Turnover rates

It's much better to look at the turnover rate of an area rather than home values, and to assess the number of transactions you're likely to gain as a function of that rate. The turnover rate can be calculated as the number of homes sold in a neighborhood over one year, divided by the total number of homes in that neighborhood.

Turnover rate = # of homes sold / total # of homes

You can find this information by looking it up in the MLS, or in tax records.

A software program called Realist makes it easier to search tax records for this information. When you're looking at the number of homes sold in your potential farm, it's important to use a polygon search (where you draw your own shape onto a map in the MLS system) instead of a wild card or neighborhood field – this will get more accurate results. Because "neighborhood" is not a drop-down menu category in most MLS listing forms, it's not uniformly documented. Some people will spell the neighborhood name wrong, or abbreviate, or not include it at all. When you search by polygon, the search covers everything within the boundaries of your shape, regardless of how it's referred to in the system.

Choosing where to farm based on turnover rate will give you better results. Where homes sell more often, you have a higher likelihood of getting a listing. Even though an area has high prices, if there is little turnover, you'll end up with fewer sales.

In choosing an area, ideally you'll want to see a 6 percent turnover rate or higher. Looking at the previous year's data will be good indicator of how many homes are likely to turn over in an area for the coming year. Sales trends can be monitored on a line graph, so as you start to see the turnover trend slowing, you might want to try farming a new area.

Average sale price

All of the above is not to say that home prices are irrelevant. You need to know the median sale price for homes in an area to be able to assess your projected ROI. Search the MLS for an area where the average sale price is a sufficient amount to match your goal, *and* there is a decent rate of turnover.

Average days on market

Another consideration that needs to go into your assessment of a potential farm area is the average number of days homes stayed on the market. A neighborhood where homes sit on the market for a long time might not be a good target as compared with an area where homes move quickly.

Often the best areas for geo-farming are those where home styles are more homogenous, because they tend to sell more quickly. In older neighborhoods where every home has unique attributes, it can take longer to find a matching buyer for your listing. Conversely, people looking in an area with mostly similar homes generally know the criteria they want, and don't require one specific house because many homes in the area meet their needs.

Also, newer neighborhoods turn over faster, because initially everyone is on the same buying cycle. Consider that people statistically move every seven to ten years. In new neighborhoods where everyone bought around the same time (when the development was brand new), they will likewise be hitting the seven-year mark at about the same time. As neighborhoods get older, subsequent sales become more staggered and turnover rates go down, because homeowners have entered the neighborhood at different times.

Another demonstrated trend is that townhouses tend to have higher turnover rates, as they typically attract larger numbers of move-up buyers. People may have a shorter living cycle in a townhome before re-entering the market, and therefore a larger volume of sales occur in areas with concentrations of these types of homes.

For an illustration of how all these factors go into determining what area to target, take a look at the spreadsheet I made when I was making my own decision:

Nieghborhood	Type	Years Built	Homes
Delgany	TH	2003-2007	192
Shadow Creek	SF	1988-1994	298
Nottingham	SF	1998-2009	421
Woodland Creek	TH	2004-2005	138
Bonaire	SF	2008-2011	178
Waterstone	TH	2004-2006	77
Gladstone	SF	1997-2000	257
Copper Marsh	SF	1998-2000	128

Nieghborhood	Targets	Cost to Mail 12x	Avg. Sales Price
Delgany	83	$747.00	$235,000
Shadow Creek	199	$1,791.00	$436,500
Nottingham	285	$2,565.00	$580,500
Woodland Creek	80	$720.00	$198,500
Bonaire	48	$432.00	$513,800
Waterstone	26	$234.00	$168,250
Gladstone	200	$1,800.00	$499,900
Copper Marsh	67	$603.00	$357,750

Nieghborhood	Avg. Comm.	# Sold Last Yr.	Turn over Rate
Delgany	$7,755	17	8.9%
Shadow Creek	$14,405	8	2.7%
Nottingham	$19,157	13	3.1%
Woodland Creek	$6,551	12	8.7%
Bonaire	$16,955	7	3.9%
Waterstone	$5,552	8	10.4%
Gladstone	$16,497	3	1.2%
Copper Marsh	$11,806	9	7.0%

Nieghborhood	Expected Sales	Expected GCI	Expected ROI
Delgany	1.7	$13,183.50	16.6
Shadow Creek	0.8	$11,523.60	5.4
Nottingham	1.3	$24,903.45	8.7
Woodland Creek	1.2	$7,860.60	9.9
Bonaire	0.7	$11,868.78	26.5
Waterstone	0.8	$4,441.80	18.0
Gladstone	0.3	$4,949.01	1.7
Copper Marsh	0.9	$10,625.18	16.6

Consider the Delgany neighborhood. As you can see from the chart, the homes in this area were built between 2003 and 2007, making them eight to 12 years old (as of the time I was making this assessment in 2015). The turnover rate in this neighborhood is very high at 9 percent.

Compare this to the Shadow Creek neighborhood, where homes were built between 1988 and 1994, making them over 20 years old. In this area, where the first cycle of turnover has already occurred, most people will now likely remain longer. And as you can see, the turnover rate in that neighborhood is only 3 percent.

The data on the Gladstone neighborhood illustrates how median home price alone should not drive your farm area selection. You might think this would be a good place to target because it has an above-average median home value for the area. However, with only 257 homes in the development and a turnover rate of only 1.2 percent, this would not be likely to yield a good return on investment.

Return on Investment

If you mail to any given area consistently for one year, you should expect to get 10 percent of the area's listings. Use this statistic to project approximately how many sales you can expect from the number of listings anticipated.

For instance, in the Delgany neighborhood, a total of 17 homes sold last year. If you plan to mail to that area for that one year, you should expect to gain 1.7 sales. From there, knowing the median sale price, as well as your cost per mailing, you can calculate how much money you would make from your efforts.

You should know how many homes you target, as well as how much it costs to send each bulk mailing. I try to keep my cost to 75 cents per house. If I multiply my cost per house times the number of houses in a mailing, I get my cost per mailing.

Cost per mailing = cost per house x # of houses in mailing

If I multiply that times twelve mailings per year, I can figure out my total cost for the year.

Mailing cost per year = cost per mailing x 12

To figure out my return on investment, I subtract how much I spend from how much I make.

ROI = GCI – Mailing cost per year

When you graph out all the factors, as in the example, you

can make an apples-to-apples comparison between different neighborhoods by calculating your anticipated ROI. Ultimately, nothing else really matters but your ROI and expected GCI. Make your decision where to locate your geo-farm based on these factors.

Size of area

How big should your farmed area be? You don't want to take on too big an area, since it costs time and money to market to your farm regularly. But, you also don't want to select an area that is too small to give you sufficient listings to make it worth your while. A rule of thumb is to should target at least 500 homes. Your farm could even be a single building containing a large number of condominium units. There isn't really a cap on how big your farm can grow, as long as your budget and time allow you to service the area with sufficient frequency and attention.

Frequency of contact is more important than the size of your target area. If you were to ask ten people for their business ten times, you will have better results than asking 100 people just once each. If a homeowner isn't thinking of selling right now, they may just toss your marketing away, and that would be a waste of your effort.

However, if you're mailing to them multiple times, two things happen. First, the consumer will start to recognize your name, and you'll develop a brand as an agent who knows that neighborhood. Second, the more often you send out marketing, the more chances you have for success. The homeowner may not be selling today, but they might be three months from now.

Competition

It's also worthwhile to see who else is already mailing in the area you're looking at. If there is someone already dominating that market, it might not be a good place for you to focus.

For example, of the neighborhoods I researched, I determined that I could receive a 26 percent ROI in the Bonaire neighborhood. That would be great, except that I happened to know that someone from my same company was already mailing to this area. Also, he actually lives there, and he's sold lots of homes there. I decided that in this case, particularly in light of the small number of homes in the area and low turnover rate, the competition was just too high and not a good investment of my time and money.

In that instance, I actually knew my competition for an area, but often that's not the case. Sometimes, I'll do a bit of sleuthing. I may ask people in the neighborhood if they're currently receiving any real estate postcards in the mail. Of course, it can be hard to know for sure. You may not know for your first year if someone else is already covering an area, or how effective you're being.

What to send, and how often

Now that you've established a geo-farm to which you'll mail at least once a month, you need to decide what to send. There are all sorts of companies out there trying to sell you marketing materials, including things like recipes, sports schedules, and seasonal/holiday items.

Don't assume that people will hold on to your marketing, especially your first mailing. It may fail to get someone's attention, particularly when they're not planning a move anytime soon. People are busy, and they don't look at what they consider junk mail.

Try not to be part of that. Give the consumer something of value, such as market statistics for the area, or recent sold comparisons. The most useful information you can provide to homeowners is real estate-related, generally in one of three categories:

- *Evidence of success*—e.g., a "just sold" card, noting percent of the listing price received, and days on the market;
- *A call to action* –e.g., announcement of buyers looking for homes, with specifics, mailed only to homes meeting the sought criteria; or
- *An invitation to your landing page*—e.g., a postcard that offers to help figure out the value of their home.

You might also send other things as a gentle reminder that you are available, with a piece of advice related to homeownership, or information on a market trend. Remember that most people are very visual, so keep your marketing consistent to strengthen your brand. Don't just send something with no value, such as a card with your branding but no content.

It's best to alternate your messages each month, rotating consistently through each of the above categories. Vendors can help you to coordinate your messaging. The additional cost of using a vendor is offset by decrease in cost per unit based the volume of postcards being sent.

Just Listed & Just Sold postcards are very powerful marketing tools. Real estate often has a popcorn effect, in which when one home goes on the market, soon after others in the same neighborhood will as well. This is a great time to demonstrate that you're an expert in the area, and gives the neighbors a taste of your professional marketing. Once the home is sold, let the neighbors know with a Just Sold card, and be sure to ask for their business.

All of your marketing should suggest that you're an expert in the area and that particular price point. It should provide examples of the ways you were able to successfully market a previous home to attract qualified buyers. Did you overcome any challenges during the transaction? Were there multiple offers? Did you receive an offer close to or above the original list price? Were you able to sell it in fewer days than the average for your market? Did you do something unique in order to market the property? These are all things that make great attention getters for your Just Sold cards.

There should also be a strong call to action, with your contact information so they can reach you. You'd be surprised by how many agents actually overlook that detail.

At the end of the year, I sort our sales by style, location, and price point to create postcards that feature anywhere from six to eight similar properties. Each card has a photo, a caption describing the property, the percent list-to-sale price, and its days on market. The reason we do not use actual listing or sales price is because it is not relevant. The consumer may have their own perception of value. What is important is how close the list price was to the sales price and how quickly the property sold.

You should also be sending these same messages out via your website and social media. Photos, stories, and testimonials from clients are very effective ways to advertise.

Frequency vs. Reach

It's important to be in touch with targets in your geo-farm

on a monthly basis, in order to become a familiar resource to them. The frequency and consistency of which you mail is more important than number of homes you reach per mailing. Some agents will contact their target farm area up to 24 times per year, or every two weeks. However, we believe this level of frequency is risky: not only are you doubling your mailing budget, but you may be in danger of alienating your target audience by annoying them. We recommend twelve mailings per year, one every month.

After twelve months (and twelve mailings), I look back to see if my targeting was successful or not. I look at turnover rates, at whether houses that did list called me, what percentage of area listings I got, and which homes sold. I gather as much information as I can to assess how I did, giving me insights from which to make business decisions for the upcoming year. Overall, mailing areas and mailing lists will remain largely the same from one year to the next, aside from dropping people who are no longer in the neighborhood. As with other strategies we talk about in this book, it's important that you commit to the area you've chosen to farm and not make any drastic changes for at least one year.

Best practices for Calls to Action

When designing the content your mailing, one important component is to include a compelling ***call to action (CTA)***—how you're asking your audience to engage, in a manner that invites them to receive value from you, and deepens their association with you and your service.

One of the best ways to frame your CTA is to make it specific. Rather than sending a card saying generally, "Homes Sold Recently in Your Neighborhood," give details indicating your success with aspects consumers care about, such as what percent of the list price you got, and how many days the home was on the market. In fact, the sale price is actually irrelevant. What matters is how close you came to doing what you said you would do, and by showcasing that success you position yourself to be the agent of choice in the future.

All your marketing pieces need to represent the level of professionalism you provide and have consistent branding. Use professional photography, and maintain some common elements between each card. This sets the tone for convincing people to trust your expertise, and to take the action you request.

One good strategy is to invite people to find out information about the price of their home by giving them a website in which to input their data. Inviting them go online and check it out for themselves is a strong call to action, and a more effective prompt than simply telling them their home's value in a mailer.

Another common approach is to send a mailer stating, "Thinking of selling?" or, "We have buyers looking for homes in your neighborhood." A much better CTA for this type of message would be to provide additional details and specificity that connects the audience with your request: "I have a homebuyer, Frank, looking for a home three to four bedrooms and two stories, in the Southview school district." Then, only send this mailer to homes matching that criteria. People are much more likely to follow up on that kind of solicitation. You want to evoke your reader's emotion and get a higher response rate.

I also like to personally invite neighbors to my open houses within my geo-farm. If there's another agent in your office with a listing in your geo-farm, ask them if it would be alright to hold an open house on their behalf.

Working with a Vendor

As we've noted, homeowners will statistically move an average of every seven years, which is very easy to track using public tax records. We can also use public records to look up how much they paid, and use automated value systems to have an idea what their home might be worth now. It doesn't make a lot of sense to market to someone who just bought their home, or who is completely upside down on their mortgage.

We want to focus our marketing efforts on those who may be ready, willing, and able to sell. Consider the reasons people decide to sell: it might be a promotion, marriage, a new addition to the family, job relocation, graduation, divorce, or death. Most real estate sales occur because of a major life change. If you were able to know when these events occur, in theory you could get in front of the sellers at just the right time.

Companies such as Core Fact and GeographicFarm.com can help you setup your farm and have automated mailing programs designed for real estate. These vendors include a Seller Landing Page to collect interested homeowners' information and provide them with an estimated value. You could also create your own postcards and drive traffic to a landing page from a company like Prime Seller Leads, or HomeValues.com

Smart Zip offers a turnkey multi-channel marketing program which includes postcards, hand written notes, and social media ads designed to target the top 20 percent of homes most likely to list, based on their predicative analytics. This is a great option for someone who doesn't have the time or know-how to narrow down their list themselves. A word of caution: by only targeting select households, you may miss out on additional opportunities. A smart way to use these services is for the specific goal of increasing the percentage of households you're targeting.

With a geo-farm, your average success rate should be about one in 2,000 contacts (this means that for every 2,000 physical pieces of mail, you will likely see one closed transaction). Vendors will try to sell you on a promised "response rate," but there can be some confusion between annual response rates and per-mailer response rates. To assess how you're doing, it's best to look at your *success rate* on an annual basis relative to how many pieces of mail you sent.

Methods of mailing

Not all mailing methods are created equal. In fact, there is some truth to the old adage "you get what you pay for." It's a good idea to consider *how* you mail when you send out your geo-farm mailings.

For your first mailing to an area, you should spend the extra money to put stamps on the envelopes, and either hand-address or print a label, so that your mail will go ***first class***. This way, you'll get the bounce-back—all the items with undeliverable addresses. Many agents don't realize that you won't get your returned mail with bulk mailing. Getting this returned mail is important, because you can use it to refine your list, fix errors, and scrub the bad addresses. If you don't do this, you could spend the next year paying for mail to go repeatedly right into the dead letter garbage.

After you've scrubbed your list, use ***business class*** to send your mailings. You won't get the bounce -back, and there is a pretty large delivery time window with this type of mail. Often, carriers will deliver all business mail on the same day of the week, so people receive a lot of junk mail all at once. This makes your fabulous postcard less likely to get noticed (and more likely to get tossed in the trash). But the price differential is pretty significant between first and business classes. Generally, it doesn't pay to use first class unless it's your first mailing to the area, or you're sending something that is time sensitive.

The third class of mail is called "Every Door Direct Mail" (EDDM), and this is what we refer to as ***bulk mail***. EDDM, as its name suggests, goes to everyone on a given carrier's route. Each piece in a bulk mailing will be considerably cheaper, but you'll need to weigh the cost-savings against the lack of specificity to your selected audience. Often, by making a targeted list, you can cut the number of people in an EDDM area in half. On the other hand, if you can pinpoint a delivery route that entirely or mostly overlaps with your targeted area, it might make sense to save money this way.

Multi-channel approach

One way to maximize the success of your geo-farm is to take a multi-channel approach to making contact with your target audience. It's best to reach out not just by mail, but also with targeted electronic ads (you can connect these from your website landing page back to the person putting in their information), as well as in-person.

Being physically present and meeting face-to-face makes a strong and lasting impression. Your marketing will be ten times more effective if you're seen out in the community. You can do so by hosting open houses in the neighborhood, or by sponsoring and/or volunteering at local community events. If it's logistically possible in your area, door-knocking is a great way to meet homeowners (see Chapter 11 for more on door-knocking).

Shannon Brooks, with Engel and Völkers (Minneapolis, MN), offers the following story about a creative approach she took to connect with her geo-farm:

"I'm a strong believer that real estate is a relationship business. It's all about the service you provide. One of my goals was to farm and door-knock with a purpose. By taking my farming and door knocking to the next level, I am able to provide a higher level of service to my local market.

"Twice a year, my team and I do a local food drive. We door-knock over 150 homes in our farm, and drop off branded donation bags. We ask all the homeowners in our farm for any non-perishable food donations they could contribute to local food shelves. We then return the following weekend to pick up the full donation bags. This annual event has grown into a fun event for my team and my vendor partners. We all participate in dropping off and collecting the bags. Leveraging my vendor partners allows us to hit more homes in less time. It also allows our vendors to participate with our team and talk to local people within our community.

"The main purpose is for me and my team to give back to our local communities. It also helps establish our brand, and allows us to get to know the people in our farm. I've shared this tactic with other agents nationally, and discovered that it can help other agents who aren't comfortable with traditional door-knocking. Once you break through that first stage of door-knocking fear, you'll never look back. It will become one of the easiest lead generation pieces you implement into your business. "

One Year + Commitment

It takes some time to begin to see a return on any of your marketing outreach efforts, and this is especially true with geo-farming. After about your eighth month of sending out your monthly mailings, you'll start to see a more consistent pattern. As with any marketing strategy that you undertake to reach beyond your sphere, you really need to give it a minimum of one year to gather sufficient information about how you are doing and what adjustments you might make. If you're not willing or able to see your efforts through for a year (and ideally, longer), you're better off not even starting a geo-farm.

Sticking with it does have its rewards. When you begin to get listings in these neighborhoods, your success rate will continue to grow as you earn the trust of your neighborhood. Once you're recognized as the expert in the area, all of your hard work will pay off.

"Farming with door-knocking has changed my business. By establishing my target areas and developing a plan, I was able to double my business. I started by investing in monthly mailers that went out to my desired sales areas. Every mailer has a call to action; it allows the homeowner to sign into a landing page and request their home's value. Once a homeowner signs into the landing page, I am notified. My team and I hand-deliver a mini CMA. This gives the homeowners and me a chance to connect. I am proving them something of value. From there I offer to return to provide a full listing presentation. Bottom line: you must put in the work. You cannot expect your system to do all the work for you. "

Shannon Brooks, Engel and Völkers

Chapter 10: Expired Listings and For-Sale-By-Owners

Expired Listings

Many books and seasoned real estate experts will tell you to go after expired listings, which have often been regarded as the second-lowest hanging fruit after your sphere of influence. Your competition knows this, and they may be going after your just-expired listing right now. While there's nothing we can do to stop them, what we can do is make sure to provide enough value that we stand out from the competition.

An expired listing is simply a seller who tried to sell their home but failed. There are a number of reasons why homes do not sell. The number one reason is price, followed by condition of the home, poor staging or photography (marketing), unavailability for showings, and market conditions such as seasonal demand. Sometimes, that reason is obvious (e.g., a home that is way overpriced, renters who do not allow showings, photos taken with a cell phone), other times it's just a matter of poor timing or narrowly missing the mark.

We can identify these potential clients by their changing status on the MLS. Many agents will reach out to them, to attempt to secure their business when they relist. I've had sellers tell me they received over 50 letters in the mail in the weeks after taking a home off the market. Some more aggressive agents will call using services such White Pages, Arch Agent, Landvoice, and Mojo Dialer powered by either RedX or Vulcan7. This would be overwhelming for anyone, and the seller may need some time to re-evaluate their needs. It's very likely they'll receive offers to relist the property at a discount. Some agents may even claim to have a buyer for them, or offer to buy the home themselves if it doesn't sell.

There are many different tactics to go after expired listings, some obviously more aggressive than others. You should do what you think is appropriate and most closely matches your style. We do not often advocate looking up people's phone numbers, or showing up at their door; but you should send them a letter or two, or maybe even three. If you do call, have a script; and call in the morning between 8 and 10 a.m. or in the afternoon between 3 and 6 p.m.

Until the property is relisted, it is a potential listing lead that should be nurtured it just like a buyer lead. My first letter introduces myself, and how we conduct business. After that, I follow up and offer tips and suggestions that have helped other sellers in the past sell their homes effectively. Many agents stop after the first mailer.

The goal in pursuing an expired listing is to stand out from the crowd, get the appointment, and secure the listing based on your unique value proposition. You want to be the first to contact, to provide seller value, to secure the appointment, and to follow up consistently until they relist (ideally with you).

Because of the huge amount of inquires expired listings draw, it is likely that the seller will interview multiple agents before deciding with whom to relist. You'll need to have your listing presentation polished. Also, don't forget to track your appointment conversion rate:

Appointment Conversion Rate = # listing contracts signed / # of appointments

My team used to do very well with expired listings, securing an average of 1 in 100 with our three-part letter series. But in the last few years, the market has shifted, and now because it's more of a seller's market, homes that don't sell usually have a good reason beyond an agent's poor marketing. There's been a shortage of inventory, and our success rate with expired listings has gone down. We continue to change and reassess our strategy, and have had success going after listings that have expired in previous years but have not since relisted.

My team's experience with expired listings represents the ongoing challenges of building an economy-proof real estate business, as well as the need for diversification of your approach. If my team had been in a position where we relied too heavily on our expired listing success, this recent change in the market would have hit us hard. Instead, we have turned our focus to other strategies which continue to yield good results.

This underscores the importance of continually tweaking your practices. All strategies need regular review—don't assume that because one approach was very successful in the past that it will always be successful.

Despite the ups and downs of the market, there will always be some agents who are able to master a strategy and make it work for them. Nick Baldwin, of Keller Williams Realty, is an agent who has elevated converting expired listings to an art form. He offers his thoughts on his team's success:

> **"Expired listings need to be treated in a different, more empathetic manner than other forms of prospecting. Think about it: having your home on the market for six months, only to have it not sell, is extremely disappointing. Equally disappointing is that the person you hired to sell your home didn't get the job done.**
>
> **An owner of an expired listing wants to know that you can understand their frustration. Your industry has let them down, and you take the blame for that. When you're speaking with a potential expired listing client, really listen. Hear their pain and frustration. Assure them that all agents are NOT created equal, and that they shouldn't give up.**
>
> **They were selling their home for a reason. They want or need to move, and you want to see that happen for them. What I say when I'm about to close the appointment is, 'Would you happen to have just 20 to 30 minutes for a cup of coffee? I can show you how my team markets homes differently so they sell quickly and for more money. If you don't like what you see or hear, we can both go our separate ways, no strings, and you got a free cup of coffee.**
>
> **My team has been extremely successful with**

this approach. Our thinking is that someone will get any given expired listing, and we try to stand out from the crowd so that we become the agents of choice in this situation."

-Nick Baldwin
Keller Williams Realty
The Baldwin Dream Team

For Sale by Owner

A For Sale by Owner (FSBO) is a seller who tried to sell their home themselves and failed. Statistically, over 80 percent of sellers who attempt to sell themselves will end up listing with a real estate agent. FSBO and expired listings are often lumped together, because you can market to them in a similar fashion.

With an FSBO, check first to make sure that the listing isn't still active in the MLS, as some homeowners will list with a FSBO service. If there is still an active listing, it may be unethical for you to contact them to offer your services.

Some of the best FSBO leads are found simply by driving around the neighborhood and spotting the hand-written *For Sale* sign in yard. You can also find FSBOs on craigslist and on Zillow under the "Make me Move category."

It's a good idea to create letters specifically for these types of listings. There are vendors you can use that will provide you with phone numbers of Expired and FSBO sellers, and they can also scrub the list for you. With this list, you can block time each day to call on them, and possibly be the first to reach them. The entire goal of your phone call should be to set up a listing appointment. You'll also want to continue to do some sort of direct mail campaign as a part of your multi-channel marketing program.

Chapter 11: Miscellaneous Engagement Strategies

Make your Open House Work for You

Open Houses have long been an effective way to appease the seller, as well as to engage potential buyers. But frankly, few sales are made at an open house, and usually the real benefit goes to the agent who is running it. An open house is great opportunity to reach an audience of 15,000 people over the three-to-four-day period prior to the open house.

The art of the open home has not been perfected by most agents. Putting out a few "open house" signs three minutes before the scheduled start time of the event is not going to produce the necessary results to make you successful. If used with purpose and consistency, an open house can serve the needs of the seller and the buyer. And perhaps most significantly, you, the agent, can register more face-to-face time engaging additional clients.

When considering an open house, make sure it is the best use of time for your business. Questions to ask yourself, or your team, include:

- Is the home in my target price and area?
- Does this event give me more visibility?
- Is this house a good representation of my personal brand?
- Is the house priced right?

Each of these questions will help you determine if this open house will benefit your business.

The Art of a Great Open House

Pulling off an open house that makes a splash requires some planning. Ideally, you'll want to allow two weeks to plan and prepare properly.

As you prepare, consider these questions:

- What is special about this listing?
- What can be used to draw attention to the open house?

Promotion

You need to promote the open house ahead of time in order to drive the greatest amount of traffic to the property. You also want to call out what is unique and compelling about the home, to attract people who are looking for these attributes.

Some options for doing so include Facebook, MLS Open House, and even national websites.

- MLS Open House. This allows other brokerages to see the open house and potentially share it with their buyers.

- ➷ Post to your brokerage website. This allows all agents within your office/brokerage to see the open house and share it with their potential buyers.
- ➷ Post to your sphere. Ask that your advocates and/or affiliates share on their pages. The spider web of connections allows a significant number additional people to see the advertisement organically.
- ➷ Realtor.com, Trulia, and Zillow can be useful to promote open houses to the general public. These sites receive a significant amount of traffic each month from buyers looking for information on local homes for sale.

Timeline

Three to seven days prior to the open house:

- ✓ Door-knock the twelve homes adjacent to the subject property. This is a great opportunity to meet new potential sellers, while inviting them to your event and asking them to bring their friends and family, or any potential buyers they know.
- ✓ Scope out where you will want to put open house signs. Signs are great for creating a buzz. Put out as many signs as possible – as many as15 to 20. There is no such thing as too many signs so long as local law allows. Place them on street corners leading to the house, as well as on nearby heavy-traffic areas, with directional arrows.

One week prior to the event:

- ✓ Hang a sign rider letting people know the time and date of the upcoming open house.

- ✓ Check all online open houses, to see what else is garnering attention that day.
- ✓ Remind the sellers to repost the Facebook event to their circle of friends and family.
- ✓ Repost on Facebook to your sphere.

Day of the event:

- ✓ 60 minutes prior to opening the door, put out multiple signs in the yard, as well as new attention-grabbing directional arrows.
- ✓ Make sure the home is ready for visitors. How does it look, is it clean? Does it smell inviting? Is there any off-putting noise, squeaky fans or loud neighboring dogs?
- ✓ Take steps to ensure you elicit the response you want from the visitors.

The Open House

It's time to open the door!

- ✓ Dress for success.
- ✓ Introduce yourself right away, engage all visitors.
- ✓ Provide handouts that create a value proposition, such as "Seven Mistakes Buyers Make." Have additional information available, but be sure to have a reason to follow up with visitors.
- ✓ Capture their information and follow up! You can use an open house feedback form, a home-buyer questionnaire, a sign-in sheet, or a drawing for lead capture.
- ✓ Ask for feedback.
- ✓ Use technology to encourage interaction. RPR

(REALTOR® Property Resource—available throughout the country, but data quality can vary depending on region) is a great resource to have up for viewing at an open house. Using neighborhood reports and the area overview can increase the time visitors spend in the house.

- ✓ Google Maps offer some additional talking points, such as schools, restaurants, and area attractions.
- ✓ Offer to send information via email for visitors to look over after leaving.
- ✓ Bring something else along to work on, for when there aren't any visitors—but don't look like you're being interrupted when people show up!

The Follow Up

You did all the work, now reap the reward.

- ↳ Send personalized emails or handwritten notes to each person you met.
- ↳ Add each registrant to your CRM and create an action plan.
- ↳ Provide the feedback to the seller.

To determine your open house success rate, look at the number of hours of open houses held over a year, compared to the number of sales. Money isn't always the measure of your investment. In the case of open houses, it's your time. Some agents will kill it with open houses; for others, they're just a waste of their time.

Door-Knocking

Does door-knocking really work? If you do a Google search of "door-knocking for real estate agents," you'll find countless success stories. Stories like Tom Mitchell with Keller Williams, who in 2013 closed $38.8 million in home sales, all from door-knocking. Or like newer agent Shannon Brooks, who closed 26 transactions her first year in business, eight of which she attributes to door-knocking.

Plain and simple: *yes,* door-knocking does work. Then why don't more agents utilize this strategy?

Because it's scary! How many times have you heard "get comfortable being uncomfortable" as a key to success? The first house I ever door-knocked, the homeowner came to the door, and I stumbled backwards and couldn't get my tongue to work. I pushed a cheesy flyer into her hand, and ran back to my car. I sat in the car half-crying and half-laughing. Fear of rejection and the initial discomfort are the most common reasons more agents don't hit the streets and engage potential customers face-to-face.

"I think some agents are scared, and think people are going to be rude and yell in your face," Tom Mitchell explains in a Keller Williams blog. He finds that nothing could be further from the truth. "People treat me with respect and are friendly – even the ones who are not interested are friendly!"

Sure, you may occasionally get a door slammed in your face rather than a foot in the door. When that happens, it helps to remind yourself that rejection is "specific and temporary," not a personal attack, according to *Business Insider*'s Max Nisen. He recommends that you shake it off and move on.

Chances are pretty good that you'll meet someone nice behind the next door. Every *no* is a step closer to a *yes*.

It isn't easy to overcome the paralyzing fear that homeowners will be ill-tempered or that rejection lies behind every door. Reminding yourself of how lucrative this prospecting method can be may help break the paralysis.

Tips for Productive Door-Knocking

Successful agents who door-knock adhere to a few key tips to follow to ensure a successful effort:

- Dress professionally, but for your market. If you sell real estate in casual Manhattan Beach, California, you don't want to wear a shirt and tie. But in New York City, you'd be wise to consider it.
- Smile.
- Step back from the door three feet or so.
- Bring something to leave behind with the homeowner—make sure it's branded with your information. RPR (REALTOR® Property Resource, provided by NAR) has some incredibly consumer-friendly home and community reports you can leave with the homeowner.
- Be target-specific. Area, style, price range and audience are important when choosing where you want to door-knock. In some markets, agents have access to data that can be helpful. For instance, Realist allows you to identify an area using a map search and then allows you to set specific criteria to find homes where the owner has lived in the house for a certain amount of time. It also gives you the original sale price, which you can use to determine their amount of equity.
- Be consistent. There's a chance that on your first time or

your tenth or your hundredth out you will end up empty handed. *Keep going!*

- Work on your script and delivery.

Scripts: Consistency Counts

If you were one of the thousands of agents that took the old Mike Ferry productivity courses years ago, you might remember his cold-calling script. Done right, the script was a business-changer for cold-callers.

It can also be effective with face-to-face prospecting. That script, now called the Just Listed Script, is available online at www.mikeferry.com/main/files/aw_just_listed_script.pdf (Tip: Don't skip any of the questions, because they all lead to the "conversation-changer" that occurs at number six.)

Here's another resource for good sales scripts: http://realtormag.realtor.org/sales-and-marketing/quick-scripts

Get familiar enough with your script that you don't sound canned, but conversational and organic. That way, you can concentrate on listening, and not on what you want to say.

Like all lead generation techniques, the results from knocking on doors takes time to show results and a successful return on investment. Remember, this is a marathon, not a sprint! It can take from two to six months to see results, so use a schedule to keep yourself on task. Tom Mitchell says he knocks four days a week, averaging 600 doors a week. The lack of instant gratification causes many agents to quit too soon. It is crucial that you commit time and consistency if you hope to reap lucrative rewards.

Then, as with all lead generation methods, the fortune is in the follow-up. Send a thank-you note about a week after a conversation with a homeowner. Add the names and notes to your CRM system and choose your action plan. Typical plans include newsletters, market update emails, additional personal touches, calls and direct mail.

"Keep in mind that whether you're a salesperson or not, you are always knocking on some kind physical or mental door, and your level of success and happiness will depend on how good you are at getting through those doors," says motivational speaker Andres Lara.

Last tip: Set a goal to knock on a specific number of doors per week as part of your larger marketing plan. Track your success and failures so you know what's working, and where you need to tweak your efforts.

Home-Buyer Seminars

In theory, buyer/seller seminars, and similar presentation-based events, are a perfect way to engage people beyond your sphere. But like many of the topics we have discussed, a successful seminar is the culmination of methods and metrics.

Why Hold a Seminar?

Developing new clients is not an easy task. However, by hosting seminars, you have an opportunity to showcase your professionalism, market knowledge and genuine desire to help your attendees navigate the home buying or selling process. A well-planned and executed seminar will deliver new prospects to your pipeline at a cheaper cost than many other engagement strategies.

Topics

What would make *you* attend a seminar? Chances are, it would need to be more inspired than, "Come Learn about the

Buying Process," or "Thinking of Selling? Come to this Selling Seminar." Be specific and innovative when picking a topic. Some ideas include:

- *Neighborhood Specific Topics:* New developments, or an expansion of an existing development, pique the interest of potential buyers. National builders love to showcase their products and will often agree to participate in seminars, as well as help recruit and register attendees.
- *Fixer-Upper Topics*: Many of the homes you show to buyers have items that need repair. Most of these fixes are easy and relatively inexpensive. However, many first-time homebuyers find these repairs daunting. Invite an inspector to explain what is important, and what isn't. Follow that advice with a handyman who can give step-by-step instructions to fix common issues.
- *Home Seller Topics:* Help sellers understand how to prepare their home to sell. I once did a neighborhood tour with six homeowners. At the time, they were not committed to selling. I invited them personally, by door-knocking, asking if they were aware what their home was worth, and if they knew how their home stacked up against homes in the area. I showed them four homes within a half-mile, and asked them to fill out a form on each. After, I asked each group to rate how their house compared to the homes I'd shown, using price, condition and curb appeal. This exercise resulted in a better-educated seller!
- *Age-Related Topics:* Age is often part of the reason people decide to buy or sell. Downsizing can be

rewarding, but also difficult. The key is to help aging clients determine the benefits of selling and assist with a transition plan tailored to their lives. Include investment advisors, estate planning attorneys, and active senior consultants to add validity to your seminar.

- *Yes, You CAN Buy a House Topics*: Geared at renters and those with credit concerns. Explain the economics of homeownership, and have a credit expert talk about overcoming credit issues such as bankruptcy or a prior foreclosure.
- *Relocating Buyers and Corporate Buyers and Sellers.* Companies in your community are always growing and shrinking. While prospecting, call on human resource departments and ask if they will give you access to their employees. If a company is hiring, they may be willing to allow you the opportunity to provide an event helping their employees identify the benefits of buying. On the other hand, a company that's downsizing has employees that may need to relocate.

Timing

The date and time of your presentation are important to consider, and will determine the attendance at your seminar. Depending on your audience, time of day and time of year will draw different crowds.

First, identify your audience. Consider the time of year, like tax time for an investor seminar, end of the school year for families, or in colder or warmer climates, consider late fall for snowbirds.

Time of day depends on your audience as well. Evenings may draw 9-to-5 workers, while Saturdays may work for second- and third-shift employees or those with families. A seminar geared toward aging homeowners may be best held during the day.

Location of Event

The location or venue of your seminar also has to target the audience you're trying to attract. Estimate attendance based on the topic and amount of promotion you plan to do for the event.

Plan to hold the seminar at a location other than your office. Potential buyers and seller are more likely to attend events held at common ground venues. They are also more likely to see the event as more valuable than "just a sales pitch."

There are many options for neutral venues, and many are inexpensive (or free). Consider churches, community centers, schools or libraries. Midrange venues include restaurants, coffee shops with ample space, and hotel meeting spaces. For higher end or specific audiences, you should consider presenting in higher end space, such as yacht clubs, country clubs and sporting facilities.

Promotion

You have the topic, the speakers, the time, and the place. Now, make sure your promotion hits its mark. Many local newspapers will run stories or calendars announcing events. Contact the newspaper and find out how to submit information. Larger businesses may be willing to post flyers on their company bulletin boards, or mention the event in their newsletter.

If you plan to pay for advertising, focus on publications

and websites that are popular with people in your target audience. For instance, when targeting first-time buyers, put ads in apartment-finder publications, or send direct mail to apartment complexes. Facebook now allows agents using its promotion tool to target more specific audiences, as well as to send reminders regarding an event.

However you promote, be sure to assess your investment relative to your anticipated return. Also, track your costs and results over time (ask event attendees where they learned about your event), so that you can know what efforts are most effective. (See Chapter 5 for more on calculating your ROI.)

The Event Itself

The actual presentation is often the component that is the hardest for agents. Think about what format will be most appealing to your prospects, and who will do the best job of covering the topic in an entertaining yet informative way.

Things to consider:

- Will you be the expert, and speak to the crowd in a lecture-style or interactive format?
- Will you bring in guest speakers and act as the moderator? (Think service providers, inspectors, credit specialists, mortgage professionals, title professionals, contractors, etc.)
- What audio-visual elements will you use?
- Will you have handouts?
- Will you offer refreshments?
- Will you and your service providers field questions from the audience?
- How will you allocate time?

In the end, you want your attendees to walk away with

some new and useful information, and you want them to associate you with the next steps they take toward buying or selling.

Be sure to capture attendee contact information, and, as always, be diligent with your efforts in following up after your event. Reach out to everyone who attended within one day, asking for their feedback on the seminar, offering to answer any additional questions that arose, and exploring where they are in their buying or selling process. Add these individuals into your database for continued follow-up, and reach out to them regularly.

Relocation

Many agents balk at paying big referral fees to relocation companies. But when you work with a good, value-added relocation company, it can be a great way of doing business.

Imagine how much you would have to spend finding a well-qualified buyer with a super-strong motivation to buy in your area, who has been pre-qualified and interviewed for their needs and wants, and *laid right in your lap*. You'd probably end up paying the equivalent of 30 or 35 percent of your commission to get this kind of client. When you work with a good relocation company, this is exactly the work that is done for you, and you simply pay them a fee at closing.

Please note the reference to a "good" relocation company. And, yes, there are some bad ones. Once the referral fee starts touching the 45 percent mark, your cost/benefit analysis will become a bit skewed. Moreover, many relocation companies require extensive and intrusive "check-ins" via email, phone or their own proprietary software/website. This can be annoying and a colossal waste of time.

On the other hand, sometimes the financial pain and frustration of working with that type of company can be worth it for a few transactions, if it means getting a foothold with an organization or business you would not otherwise have. Once you have the organizational connection, you can receive years of referrals. Make sure you take a look at the *big* picture when deciding if working with relocation companies is right for you.

And if you choose to incorporate relocations into your business, we recommend using a radical approach. Conventionally, working with a relocation company is simple. You get a lead, you follow up with the prospect and help them buy or sell a home. At the same time, you're reporting back to the relocation company, and at a successful closing, their referral fee is taken from your commission. That's working downstream from the relocation company. Simple, boring, and predictable. My dad used to say: "Even a dead fish can swim downstream."

What if we were to work upstream from relocation companies? Be a partner in their success as well as your own. Start making relationships with CEOs and HR Managers in small to medium-sized businesses around your area. Go to functions where these people might be in attendance. Serve on the board of a local charity, participate at a club, and join local business groups like the Chamber of Commerce or the Downtown Council. These are all great ways to serve your community and come in contact with other business leaders.

Go through your database and look at any member who might be in one of these positions, or might know someone in such a position. Use all of your connections to gain access to the small and medium-sized businesses in your area. Often, these companies are big enough to have a relocation or recruiting need, but not large enough that they have an established relationship with a relocation company. Make sure you ask right away if the company you are pursuing does, in fact, already have a relationship with a relocation company. Stepping on the toes of an existing relationship might put you further back than when you started.

There are so many businesses that rely on an educated and specialized workforce for success. Whether it's experienced plastics workers to make microscopic medical device parts, or software engineers fluent in the programming language of Haskell, there are countless instances when businesses need to do a broad regional, nationwide, or even worldwide search to fill a position. These specialized talent needs are no longer the exclusive terrain of large multi-national corporations, but could as easily arise for the 12-person software company at the end of your block.

Don't be just another real estate agent to these companies. Become a recruiting ally. Become an essential engine in their growth and development. Sit down with the decision-makers at these companies, and see how you can help grow their company by attracting the right employees to the area in which they are located.

In 2004, I served on a committee at the University of Minnesota raising money for a new Cancer and Biomedical Research Facility. (How do you get on such a board, you might ask? Call up the fundraising and foundation arms of your local institutions. They usually jump at the chance for more volunteers.) As luck would have it, I shared my time on the committee with the HR Director at a plastic extrusion company in my area. We were placed on the same sub-committee, so we had the opportunity to work closely together.

During one of our meetings, she mentioned that they were having a tough time finding local workers for the skilled level of plastic extrusion techniques required in the making of precise medical devices. She also noted that a similar company had just moved from Memphis to Europe, leaving a bunch of these skilled workers unemployed in that area, but that none of them wanted to move to Minnesota because of our weather. I told her, "I have a plan that could help."

We met a week later in her offices and charted a plan. I would go to Memphis and meet with the workers this company was trying to recruit. My plan was not to talk about the new job potential, but rather to talk about lifestyle and housing in my area. It was not an easy sell, as our housing prices were almost twice that of their current market, and the cold winters were a serious negative. I brought along my projector and some great videos about our area and what we do for fun, as well as t-shirts, baseball caps and other swag from local attractions and sports teams.

We were successful in getting three out of every five goal recruits to take an informational trip to our area. Eventually, we were able to convince 78 percent of all of those who made the trip to move to our area to take the job – which also came with a healthy pay raise.

Through my efforts, the company was getting the workers they needed. They eventually hired 48 people over the 18 months I was helping them; by comparison, they had successfully hired only four people through their own recruiting in the previous 12 months. I was able to help 22 of these people buy a home in my area, and got a small commission from another 12 who rented apartments. Four others rented apartments, with my help, where no commission was being paid, and another ten people bought a home without my help (you can't win them all).

It's important to note that all of my trips to Memphis (seven in all), all the swag, all of the videos, all of the hotel stays and expenses were mine, and mine alone. The plastic extrusion company I was working with didn't pay a dime. Moreover, when these workers would come to town, I would pick them up at the airport and drive them to their hotel. I'd always have lavish gift baskets waiting in their rooms, and I'd have baskets full of toys and electronics for their kids if they came along on the trip. Every night, I'd take them out to great local restaurants. I'd hire nannies to take the kids to water parks, amusement parks, zoos, science museums, or swimming in area lakes, while their parents and I looked at houses or neighborhoods.

Fundamentally, I made them feel like VIPs during the time they were with me, and I took care of their needs and wants. While they visited my area, I'd made sure they saw the best we had to offer. Even if they eventually decided not to take the job in my area, they were going to go away being big fans of both the area and me.

Early on in this process, I told the plastic extrusion company that they would be well-served working with a local relocation company. There is so much that a good relocation company can add to the process of recruiting and moving a new hire from one city to another. This company had never worked with a relocation company before, and they were hesitant to do so. I coordinated a meeting between them and a great relocation company I had worked with many times in the past. The meeting went great! The relocation company set up a system to help the workers moving to my area, and gave me a lot of support to make the process easier. It was a perfect relationship.

And guess what? Even though the relocation company, offered me a very low referral fee out of appreciation for my service, I insisted on paying them their full 35 percent fee. I did not want to create an incentive to for the relocation company to bring in different agents to make more revenue from this client in future transactions.

Further, I wanted to do the *opposite* of what the relocation company thought any normal real estate agent would do—I wanted to *swim upstream*. Instead of being one of the typical everyday real estate agents with whom this relocation company worked, complaining about the referral fee and just about everything else, I was the agent of their dreams.

The relocation company managers had my business card pinned to their cubical walls. I became the model real estate agent with whom this relocation company wanted to work. Instead of being the downstream agent who was constantly looking for a referral and complaining about referral fees, I became the upstream agent who was bringing business to the relocation company, and was seen as a partner. This is the least stressful and most profitable way to work relocation.

The lessons that are taught here about working in relocation span all of the methods of business creation we regularly recommend:

- Be different. If everyone expects you to *zig*, then *zag* instead.
- Don't just go beyond customer expectations; go 100,000 miles beyond it.
- Bring on smart and capable partners. You can do far more as a team, and you're better off with 20 percent of a million-dollar operation than 100 percent of a

$100,000 operation.

- Don't be greedy. Make money for everyone around you, maybe even more than you make for yourself.
- Have fun. Enjoy working with the team you have assembled, and enjoy the work you do. Fun and excitement are infectious and everyone wants to be a part of it.

True in the real estate business...true in any business... true in life.

Chapter 12: Apps to help you save time

The real estate industry is always evolving, and it's no secret that the internet has changed the way we do business. The internet caused a paradigm shift in the industry, in that agents are no longer the sole guards of listing data. Consumers are more informed than ever, but still need a knowledgeable guide through the real estate transaction.

Technology is an indisputable boon to our work, but it can become distracting. Agents get stuck in the mindset that they need a particular technology in order to achieve their goal. They'll spend more time trying to learn and implement a new product or application than focusing on money-making activities.

There really is no point to having a fancy CRM system if you're not going to pick up the phone and call your clients. Watch out for apps claiming to solve a problem that doesn't actually exist!

Here are some of our favorite pieces of technology, websites, apps, and programs that really can help you save time, and solve real problems:

- First and foremost you need a **smart phone!** The ability to have access to information, and to communicate via multiple channels at anytime, anywhere is crucial to your success. We live in the *now* generation, and getting back to someone tomorrow isn't going to cut it anymore. There are tons of great apps out there. Our favorites are Waze for GPS, email, Facebook, and a local home search app to look up properties on the go. And don't forget that the primary function of a phone is to *call* people.

- Implement a **contact relationship management system**.

  The concept is actually quite simple. You've got a big list of contacts: your database. You need to reach out to them regularly in order to stay top of mind. But how are you ever going to remember to call that past client from several years back? Or when the last time was that you did so? If only there was a system to remind you…

  Ah yes, the *contact relationship management system!* With a CRM, such as Contactually, you're able to apply rules to each of your categories of contacts. Each day, when you log in for the power hour that you've blocked for working on your database, the system will prompt you to follow up with the people you've told it to remind you about. A system like this can make simplified work of the Substantive Contacts Number you calculated in Chapter 5, and all you have to do to remember is look at your calendar.

- Are you missing addresses for people in your database? Minnesota REALTOR® Thang Holt with Keller Williams Integrity Lakes suggests using Postable, or a simple Google doc form to request an update of their contact information. Thang says: "The holidays are a great opportunity to reach out to everyone and get their updated mailing addresses for holiday cards. It is very non-intrusive and people like getting holiday greetings." Companies such as Postable and Touchnote make creating and distributing custom cards to your sphere of influence easy and fun.

- Hello Bond (bond.co) allows you to send personalized (robotic) hand-written notes, on-demand, electronically. Never worry about finding a card, having stamps on hand, or remembering to go to the post office. Everything is customizable, from the stationery down to the handwriting, and they handle all of the shipping for you.
- Don't have time to **monitor your social media channels** to see when someone may be ready to buy or sell? Mention is a tool that you can use to actively track conversations with your network. 74 percent of adults are using social media, making it a good tool to stay on top of relevant conversations. You can add value with personable contributions to conversations through Mention. You'll be at the top of your most important buyers' and sellers' minds.
- Have you ever felt **overwhelmed by e-mails**? Most of us get hundreds of emails a day, often coming in faster than you can read, respond, or delete them. Sanebox is a tool that keeps your inbox organized. With an updated and organized inbox, qualified and hot opportunities will rise to the top more easily than before. Sanebox provides a painless way to know what's important in your inbox, so those messages don't get lost with all of the promotional junk you've been getting. While you may never achieve inbox zero, since you're going to be so productive and working on so many transactions, you'll at least stay sane. While you're at it, head on over to wisestamp.com and create your own professional email signature.

- Looking for **ideas for your next blog post**? There are millions of pieces of content published every day. Some stuff out there is awesome, but as you know, a lot of it is a waste of time. Buzzsumo analyzes and shows what content is performing the best based on the topics searched. You'll be able to see the most relevant and best content to send out to your network.
- Don't fret over the **design of your next brochure** - there are great solutions available online for cheap! 99designs.com allows designers to bid for your job, and depending on how much you offer, you may get many designs to pick from. This service is great for creating logos! You can also go over to Fiverr.com where for just $5 someone out there will do pretty much anything you can think of. There are extra fees for additional features, and you certainly get what you pay for. We did two rounds on Fiverr to come up with the image to use for our Kickstarter campaign for this book. (Though once we reached our funding goal, we hired a professional to design the actual cover.)
- **Automate your business expense tracking** with the Deductr app. Krista Clark, with Century 21 Signature Real Estate in Newton, IA, snaps photos of her receipts and logs her mileage with Deductr. This helps her save time, now she never has to worry about lost receipts or missing expenses come tax season. Her accountant must love her!

Conclusion

M^3-Powered Success

In creating this book, we came together from diverse backgrounds within the real estate industry. Together, our experience encompasses a range including residential and commercial sales, development, mortgage, title and investment. We have each been immersed in the role of residential real estate agent, and know the nuances of this arena from the inside, having made plenty of our own mistakes. We've also each worked in a coaching capacity with both new and experienced agents. We have witnessed others' struggles, watched as individuals put their own spin on our suggestions, and identified what is most helpful to creating success in the real estate profession.

If we were to define what keeps agents from the success they seek in this profession, based on the thousands of people we've worked with, spoken to, coached, consulted, and been ourselves, it comes down not to any one specific trick to master, but more to the lack of a holistic and thoughtfully planned approach to one's business.

The most important thing you can do to create your own success as a real estate agent is to incorporate a multi-tiered process that addresses the entire scope of your business. Start by adopting a mindset that embraces your role as CEO of your real estate business, encompassing all that this title requires, including yearly business planning, fiscal leadership and management, and long-range goal-setting. Implement regular practices to hone your focus and skills.

Next, you need to get clear about your specific business goals, and break these down into detailed action steps that will provide you with a master to-do list for your entire upcoming year. Record this quantified plan in a calendar or contact management system, and follow it religiously for the entire year.

Finally, synthesize your calendar of substantive contact goals with the strategies you choose to utilize in your business. Refer regularly back and forth between the metrics of your daily business and your strategic objectives. Track your actions and your results, draw conclusions, and refine your approach as you move through your year. Most of all, do not abandon what you start, and hold yourself accountable for meticulous follow-through for a minimum of one year.

We've said a number of times that there's no magic bullet to get you to the top of the real estate profession. It requires good, old-fashioned work, but possibly not the kind of work you're currently doing. You don't need to spin your wheels chasing a volatile market. You can have a sane life, where others help you manage your time, you provide yourself a steady paycheck, and there is reliability to your success. The ebb and flow of your own sales pattern does not need to drive a fear-based erratic response. You can foster authentic relationships that feed you and your business.

We thought of concluding this book with a fictionalized

account of what a typical week-in-the-life would look like for a successful agent utilizing our M^3 process, in order to help you visualize how you might structure your own life. But we soon realized that there really isn't such a thing as "typical," and that each person's week is going to look very unique, based on each individual life. Some of you are relatively new to your business, perhaps single, with no children or dependents. Your day will look very different than those of you who have been working in the field for 15 years, and are supporting a family with school-age children. Some of you may be single parents, or have extended family obligations, or are responsible to another business or profession. Some are part-time, some full-time; some live in cities, some in more rural areas; some are in their 20s, some approaching retirement age. You get the idea.

The beauty of our approach, though, is that it is designed to be tailored specifically to *you.* There's no need to set aside what you need for the sake of your work. Rather, it's precisely the point that getting what you need is the only way for everything *to* work. *You* set your earnings goal; *you* decide on your best business methods; *you* calculate what you need to do each day, week, month; and *you* figure out the time it takes to make it happen. Then, you are accountable *to you* for following through on the plan you design.

You *can* do this. You *can* enjoy sustainable and predictable, successful results in your real estate business. And hopefully, when you have attained this goal, you'll also reconnect with the reasons you entered this profession in the first place, and be free to truly enjoy what you do.

Acknowledgments

We could not have written this book without the financial support of our Kickstarter backers. We thank:

Russel Branjord
Chad Kingbay
Brent Adams
Nick Kelvie
Corey Collins
Chris Long
Tasha Soundara
Jeff Steeves
Bofei Cao
Bryn Erickson
Ben Nelson
Contactually
SaundersDailey
Andrew Biscay
Amanda Galindo
Michael Doyle
Collin Vold
Lee Aldrich
Tim Nichols
Franco Nicolich
Sarah Willems
Bethany Nelson
Eric Stegemann
Cassandra Jacobson
Jason Hudoba
Sarah Huffman
Tyler Fairchild
Shannon Brooks
Ann Gunderson
Ryan Bokros
Colton Pratt
Kelly Sullivan
Jim Bohanon
Mandy Eckman
Margaret Doyle